# Police
# Performance Appraisals

## A Comparative Perspective

# Advances in Police Theory and Practice Series

## Series Editor: Dilip K. Das

# Police Performance Appraisals

## A Comparative Perspective

Serdar Kenan Gul and Paul E. O'Connell

CRC Press
Taylor & Francis Group
Boca Raton London New York

CRC Press is an imprint of the
Taylor & Francis Group, an **informa** business

CRC Press
Taylor & Francis Group
6000 Broken Sound Parkway NW, Suite 300
Boca Raton, FL 33487-2742

First issued in paperback 2019

ISBN-13: 978-1-4398-3946-1 (hbk)
ISBN-13: 978-0-367-86532-0 (pbk)

This book contains information obtained from authentic and highly regarded sources. Reasonable efforts have been made to publish reliable data and information, but the author and publisher cannot assume responsibility for the validity of all materials or the consequences of their use. The authors and publishers have attempted to trace the copyright holders of all material reproduced in this publication and apologize to copyright holders if permission to publish in this form has not been obtained. If any copyright material has not been acknowledged please write and let us know so we may rectify in any future reprint.

| Library of Congress Cataloging-in-Publication Data |
| --- |

Gül, Serdar Kenan.
    Police performance appraisals : a comparative perspective / Serdar Kenan Gul and Paul O'Connell.
        p. cm.
    Includes bibliographical references and index.
    ISBN 978-1-4398-3946-1
    1. Police--Personnel management--United States. 2. Police--Personnel management--Turkey. 3. Police--Rating of--United States. 4. Police--Rating of--Turkey. 5. Police administration--United States. 6. Police administration--Turkey. I. O'Connell, Paul E. II. Title.

HV7936.P47G85 2013
363.2'2--dc23                                                                          2012019860

**Visit the Taylor & Francis Web site at**
**http://www.taylorandfrancis.com**

**and the CRC Press Web site at**
**http://www.crcpress.com**

# Contents

# Series Preface

While the literature on police and allied subjects is growing exponentially its impact upon day-to-day policing remains small. The two worlds of research and practice of policing remain disconnected even though cooperation between the two is growing. A major reason is that the two groups speak in different languages. The research work is published in hard-to-access journals and presented in a manner that is difficult to comprehend for a layperson. On the other hand the police practitioners tend not to mix with researchers and remain secretive about their work. Consequently, there is little dialogue between the two and almost no attempt to learn from one another. Dialogue across the globe, amongst researchers and practitioners situated in different continents, is of course even more limited.

I attempted to address this problem by starting the IPES, www.ipes.info, where a common platform has brought the two together. IPES is now in its 15th year. The annual meetings that constitute most major annual events of the organization have been hosted in all parts of the world. Several publications have come out of these deliberations and a new collaborative community of scholars and police officers has been created whose membership runs into several hundreds.

Another attempt was to begin a new journal, aptly called *Police Practice and Research: An International Journal*, PPR, that has opened the gate to practitioners to share their work and experiences. The journal has attempted to focus upon issues that help bring the two on a single platform. PPR is completing its 10 years in 2009. It is certainly an evidence of growing collaboration between police research and practice that PPR, which began with four issues a year, expanded into five issues in its fourth year, and now, it is issued six times a year.

Clearly, these attempts, despite their success, remain limited. Conferences and journal publications do help create a body of knowledge and an association of police activists but cannot address substantial issues in depth. The limitations of time and space preclude larger discussions and more authoritative expositions that can provide stronger and broader linkages between the two worlds.

It is this realization of the increasing dialogue between police research and practice that has encouraged many of us—my close colleagues and I connected closely with IPES and PPR across the world—to conceive and implement a new attempt in this direction. I am now embarking on a book series, *Advances in Police Theory and Practice*, that seeks to attract writers from all parts of the world. Further, the attempt is to find practitioner contributors. The objective is to make the series a serious contribution to our knowledge of the police as well as to improve police practices. The focus is not only in work that describes the best and successful police practices but also one that challenges current paradigms and breaks new ground to prepare a police for the 21st century. The series seeks for comparative analysis that highlights achievements in distant parts of the world as well as one that encourages an in-depth examination of specific problems confronting a particular police force.

Serdar Kenan Gul and Paul O'Connell's *Police Performance Appraisals: A Comparative Perspective* does just that. This book explores best practices in terms of the development and use of personal performance appraisals by police organizations. It examines the performance appraisal systems of the Ankara and Toledo police departments in order to explore the degree to which both departments' performance appraisal systems include factors that are recognized as important components of the performance appraisal process. It also considers whether the type of appraisal system (traditional versus modern) matters in terms of affecting the officers' satisfaction with the performance appraisal system of their departments and it questions whether field and command officers' perceptions of the performance evaluation instruments in their departments differ from those of their subordinates. The nature of the relationship between the officer's perception of the appraisal system and the officer's rank is examined while controlling for an officer's level of education, gender, age, and years of service. This study employs both qualitative and quantitative methodologies. Such a comparative view allows us to differentiate universal policing performance traits or practices from those that are culturally specific. Also, a comparison of traditional and community policing philosophies in these two organizations may help us explain how different organizational structures influence officer's attitudes toward the performance appraisal system. These findings provide insights to guide efforts to design better appraisal systems. Insights from this study may also contribute to nationwide assessments of evaluation practices and standards for police organizations.

It is hoped that through this series it will be possible to accelerate the process of building knowledge about policing and help bridge the gap between the two worlds—the worlds of police research and police practice. This is an invitation to police scholars and practitioners across the world to come and join in this venture.

**Dilip K. Das, PhD**
*Founding President*

*International Police Executive Symposium, IPES, www.ipes.info*

*Founding Editor in Chief, Police Practice and Research: An International Journal, PPR, www.tandf.co.uk/journals*

# Foreword

Every well-run organization needs the ability to closely direct its personnel and to assess the quantity and quality of work being performed. This is particularly true in the field of policing, where officers are not only required to master basic skills, but to continually improve upon them and to adapt to a rapidly changing work environment. Personnel performance appraisals therefore serve a critical function.

Most modern police organizations recognize this and are now critically examining their personnel appraisal practices. Increasingly, they are making necessary modifications in light of the dynamic nature of modern policing. This book provides a very thorough overview of the history and best practices associated with this evaluation process while highlighting the essential elements of an effective performance appraisal system.

Personnel performance appraisal is essential to ensure that an organization has the capacity to carry out its mission successfully. Unfortunately, it is often not easy to develop and implement the right system for a particular agency, particularly in police organizations where outputs are often intangible.

*Police Performance Appraisals: A Comparative Perspective* is a useful book for police management that combines theory and practice from two different countries, Turkey and the USA. The Turkish National Police (TNP) has undergone a vast positive change during the past twenty years. Public confidence in the Turkish Police has been increasing steadily since 1990. 78% of the public had confidence in Turkish Police in 2010; whereas, it was 62.5% in 1990. This is clearly the result of investments in human resources, as well as equipment, vehicles and physical facilities. The development of personnel has not only resulted in higher levels of personal work performance, but has enhanced the overall capacity, reputation and effectiveness of the TNP.

In recent years, the transformation of the TNP has been accelerated by scholars like Dr. Gul. They have studied and combined traditional policing practices with the modern policing techniques of other developed countries. With the sponsorship of the TNP, Dr. Gul, like many of his colleagues, has gained valuable experience and has developed a deep understanding of core police practices. Dr. Gul and Dr. O'Connell bring that understanding to bear on an often overlooked area of policing, the fair and accurate appraisal of personnel performance within police organizations.

Therefore this book has an international dimension, having Turkish and American perspectives grounded in a rich literature and many years of practical experience since Dr. Gul and Dr. O'Connell both served as police officers for many years prior to their academic careers. This is what makes this book a unique tool for police departments, criminal justice academic programs, police professionals, scholars and students.

This book will help police managers who aim to transform their organizations. It will help organizations move from a traditional management mindset towards more modern practices applied in successful organizations. It will also help managers who wish to keep their organizations at the cutting edge of a rapidly developing field.

The act of policing a community or a nation is a critically important function. May we continue to learn from one another.

To a peaceful World!

**Mehmet Kiliclar**
*Governor and General Director of Turkish National Police*
*Ankara, Turkey*

# Foreword

"The Turkish National Police is a learning organization." It was the savvy observation of an Ohio Police Chief during the first of a number of our law enforcement trips to Turkey between 2004 and 2008. Through the content and insights contained within *Police Performance Appraisals: A Comparative Perspective*, Dr. Gul and Dr. O'Connell continue to substantiate the accuracy of that observation.

As anyone involved in business management assuredly knows, the foundation for operating successfully depends upon the people you engage in your operation. A great proportion of management literature focuses on what Jim Collins metaphorically referred to as "putting the right people on the bus." But, once we have our people on our bus, how do we know they are doing their job we hired them to do? How do we know roles are being performed substantially? How do we know agreed upon goals and objectives are being effectively achieved? How do we know unacceptable actions are not being unwittingly engrained? How do we know employees understand their roles and organizational expectations? How do we know employees have the opportunity to input their perspectives? As Dr. Gul and Dr. O'Connell deliberate, adopting policies for judging and evaluating our people is paramount to achieving organizational excellence.

A unique aspect of Dr. Gul's and Dr. O'Connell's work is the international comparative nature of studying police performance appraisal systems from two major police departments from two different countries. Comparing and contrasting are powerful methodologies to surfacing "best practices." As the authors note, bi-country comparative analysis allows one to differentiate universal police practices from culturally specific police practices. Both are useful educational perspectives. Both have "value-adding" power to our mental expansion pursuits.

*Police Performance Appraisals: A Comparative Perspective* is organized in content and approach such that this unique book should become a standard text in Police Academies, and University Criminal Justice Academic Programs. Police Leadership and Management curricula pragmatically bias toward books which find marriage between balancing theory and practice. Through applied, empirical research, useful case studies surface, because information is grounded in real-life laboratory settings, that is, functioning Law Enforcement Agencies.

Explored within this text are the on-going philosophical tensions between Police Leaders who emphasize traditional policing tactics versus those who lean toward implementation of community policing practices. Conceptual verbiage used in the book is "traditional versus modern" systems of appraising performance. Proactive and reactive policing applications are not mutually exclusive, but Dr. Gul and Dr. O'Connell serve to challenge, "Are we accurately reflecting our departmental philosophy and mission by assuring personnel evaluation systems and processes mirror and measure that agency-specific philosophy and mission?"

In Ohio during the late 1980s, we developed and implemented our Police Executive Leadership College (PELC). In explaining to business leaders the value and need for PELC, I often would note, "These Police Chiefs operate multi-million dollar business organizations." The intention of the intensive PELC education program was/is to introduce a number of organizational management practices into the repertoire of Police Command Staffs. Included is a comprehensive and well-grounded police performance appraisal system, paramount to achieving operational efficiencies. Just like well operated corporate businesses, an effective "multi-million dollar" police organization requires adoption and confidence in policies, processes, and systems to evaluate the agencies' most valued asset, the police personnel.

I had the good fortune of meeting Dr. Serdar Kenan Gul while he was a Doctoral Student at Kent State University. The Turkish National Police is an organization of some 225,000 personnel. To their great credit, the TNP sent 200 of their "best and brightest" to the United States to enroll in graduate programs. Additional TNP officers enrolled in other countries' Universities. Ohio was most fortunate because a number of these "best and brightest" Officers enrolled at Kent State University, Ohio. They became Colleagues and they cemented as life-long Friends. This international educational effort, a systematic way to learn and absorb the best police practices of many countries, was principally the vision of the General Directorate of the Turkish National Police.

These TNP Officers/KSU Graduate Students developed a strong and personal relationship with the Police Chief at Kent State University, Chief John Peach. A man of vision, leadership, and consummate diplomacy, Chief Peach led our Ohio law enforcement efforts toward developing great professional and friendship relationships between the two countries' Officers and Families. As Professor Omar Alomari of the Ohio Department of Public Safety noted, "We are engaged in 'soft power' efforts to strengthen our countries' bonds, and thus, safety."

Congratulations to Dr. Gul and Dr. O'Connell for advancing policing management practices, and for centering focus on continued professionalizing of our People. Perpetuating the value of "Learning Organizations," particularly across the divides of continents and cultures, is an undertaking worth committing.

Tesekkur Ederim. Thank you.

**Todd Wurschmidt, PhD, CAE, CFRE**
*1985–2008 Executive Director*
*Ohio Association of Chiefs of Police*
*2009–Present Executive Director*
*Law Enforcement Foundation of Illinois*

# About the Authors

**Serdar Kenan Gul, PhD,** received a BS degree in criminal justice from the Turkish National Police Academy (TNPA) in 1996; an MS degree in public management from Gazi University, Ankara, Turkey, in 2001; an MA degree in criminal justice from the Department of Justice Studies at Kent State University, Kent, Ohio, in 2003; and a PhD degree from the Political Science Department at Kent State University in 2007. Dr. Gul has published many articles and book chapters and coauthored the following books: *Kamu Kurumlarinda Performans Yonetimi* [*Performance Management in Public Sector*], Ankara, Seckin, 2008; *Guvenlik Yonetimi* [*Security Management*], Ankara, Seckin, 2010; and *Sucun Olcumu* [*Measurement of Crime*], Ankara, Adalet, 2010. His research interests include police management, performance appraisal, comparative criminal justice, and quantitative research methods. After working at different units of the Turkish National Police Organization as a ranking officer for almost 15 years, Dr. Gul is currently an associate professor and director of the Security Management Research Center at TNPA. He teaches Human Resources Management, Public Administration, and Police Management courses at the College of Security Sciences and Comparative Policing graduate course at the Institute of Security Sciences at TNPA. He is also editor for the *Turkish Journal of Police Studies*, a peer-reviewed quarterly published scientific journal.

**Paul O'Connell, PhD, JD,** has been a full-time member of the criminal justice faculty at Iona College in New Rochelle, New York, since 1994. He received his PhD from CUNY where his doctoral thesis was *The History and Development of the Compstat Model of Police Management* (2002). Dr. O'Connell began his professional career in criminal justice in 1981, serving the New York City Police Department (NYPD) first as a police officer, and then as a police academy instructor, in-service trainer, and curriculum developer. After receiving an MPA and JD, he worked as a trial attorney with the firm of Cummings & Lockwood in Stamford, Connecticut. He is the former associate dean of the School of Arts and Science and former chair of Iona College's Criminal Justice Department. He teaches at both the undergraduate and graduate levels, conducts funded research, and lectures widely on the topics of police performance measurement, integrity management, and law enforcement training systems. He is the author of *Performance-Based Management for Police Organizations*, Waveland, 2007. Dr. O'Connell is a senior public safety consultant with the International City/County Management Association (ICMA) and has provided consulting services to a variety of government agencies, including assessment of existing policing policies and practices, and development of proactive management strategies. Over the years, he has collaborated with the Center for Technology in Government (Albany, New York), Giuliani Partners (New York, New York), and the Center for Society, Law and Justice (University of New Orleans). He is a participant in the Fulbright Specialists Program, Council for the International Exchange of Scholars (CIES).

# 1
# WHY APPRAISE PERFORMANCE?

An employee performance appraisal is one of the most frustrating rituals of today's workplace. Very few people enjoy preparing them. Fewer still enjoy having their performance appraised. Employees and managers alike seem to distrust and avoid them. However, the continuous demand for quality and outstanding customer service makes the employee performance evaluation a vital tool for the survival of the organization. The key to an organization's success is its ability to accurately gauge the relative strengths and weaknesses of each of its employees and set reasonable performance goals. Organizations must be adept at measuring, predicting, and guiding the performance of their employees. Additionally, employees need to feel they can make valuable contributions to the organization, while advancing their personal skills and responsibilities within the organization. Only through an effective system of employee performance evaluations can the staff be guided for development and improvement (Krug, 1998).

Unfortunately, performance appraisals themselves are often flawed and the evaluation process as a whole is generally viewed as merely a necessary evil. There is a large body of literature that has identified various limitations of performance assessment systems, such as "inflated ratings, lack of consistency, and the politics of assessment" (Catano, Darr, & Campbell, 2007, p. 201). Many police professionals simply "view employee performance evaluation as one of the useless trappings of bureaucracy" (Kramer, 1998, p. 1). Managers reluctantly perform their duty of preparing annual performance reviews for their subordinates, but evaluations are rarely candid or useful. All too frequently, supervisors try not to offend, not to say "too much," and couch their true impressions in vague generalities or generic statements that fail to convey their true opinions. Employee evaluations are typically either quite brief or laced with nonspecific statements that fail to capture or convey the true sense of individual performance. In other words, these types of evaluations are of very little use.

Rarely does any meaningful discussion take place in connection with the evaluation process. Organizations typically do a poor job of communicating personal performance expectations, evaluators receive little training, direction, or advice in proper evaluation methods, and post evaluation meetings with ratees are often conducted in a perfunctory and awkward manner. The prevailing attitude among supervisors and employees toward personnel evaluations seems to be "Let's not talk too much about them. Let's just get them done!"

In the business world, budgets are set well in advance of annual performance reviews. When it comes to annual monetary bonuses or salary raises, therefore, the "pot of gold" to be distributed among employees is predetermined. Managers performing appraisals of their personnel are normally told in advance how many employees can be considered "exceptional," and how many individuals should receive the average bonus amount. So the number of slots for each level is set in advance. All that remains is to determine who fits into each slot. Months later, the appraisal process begins. Managers then begin to review their personnel within those parameters, but the entire process loses credibility. Information is being shaped to fit decisions that have already been made. Everyone within the organization knows that all of the truly important decisions have already been made.

Clearly, the problems associated with performance appraisals occur in both the private and public sectors. Police organizations, in particular, have traditionally struggled with the employee evaluation process. Perhaps it is the understandable result of the civil service system itself, where vague consequences exist for subpar performers, combined with a dearth of tangible rewards for top performers. Perhaps it stems from internal resistance, caused by hierarchical and paramilitary structures and an organizational culture that strongly values loyalty and esprit de corps. Police organizations typically do not openly criticize themselves or their personnel, preferring instead an informal but equally effective system of rewards and punishments. Rarely will there be a paper trail. It is generally easier for a police field commander to simply transfer a troublesome officer, rather than documenting unacceptable behaviors and proceeding with formal disciplinary action. Seasoned police officials in any law enforcement agency would generally agree that the less "trouble" formally identified within a police command, the better. Newly hired police officers are routinely advised by veteran colleagues to "keep a low profile." In other words, probationary officers are informally advised to simply "fit in" and to attract neither excessive positive nor negative attention for their work behavior.

Supervisors, for their part, generally wish to avoid the paperwork required to properly document their subordinates' exceptionally good or exceptionally poor work performance. Generally speaking, it is far easier for a supervisor to rate all employees as merely "average." Even more troublesome is the supervisor who simply prefers not to identify any problems within the ranks. This type of supervisor prefers not to hear "bad news" regarding personnel, choosing instead to consider all employees as "above average" or "superior," without any form of inquiry or meaningful discernment into the actual quality or quantity of work being performed. While this situation is rare, it does occur within police organizations (as well as in other public agencies). In addition to being a complete abdication of supervisory authority, this constitutes nonfeasance of an essential management duty that creates an atmosphere that is ripe for corruption and police misconduct. Once the rank-and-file officers recognize that the performance appraisal system lacks objectivity and credibility, they will become skeptical and disenfranchised. In essence, why should one expend any real effort in performance when the evaluation system is "a joke"? Not surprisingly, research has shown that faulty performance assessments have "negative longitudinal effects on overall job satisfaction" and upon organizational commitment (Catano et al., 2007, p. 201).

Performance appraisal is therefore considered to be one of the most vexing and troubling areas of law enforcement human resource management (Allen & Mayfield, 1983; Kane, Bernardin, & Wiatrowski, 1995; Wolfer & Baker, 2000).

## A New Era of Policing

Times have changed dramatically, though, in recent years. Since the early 1990s, police organizations have developed the ability to use timely and accurate data to guide their operations. Part of that process entails setting organizational, unit, and individual performance goals or work targets, then measuring the relative degree of progress made toward stated goals. Police organizations across the world are now experiencing new operational pressures. Today, they are dealing with demands for greater fiscal responsibility, operational transparency, and personal accountability. A "business as usual" approach to policing is no longer possible. Police managers need to appreciate the complexity and dynamics of policing (Jones, 2008). They also need to possess new and varied skills.

In particular, they need the ability to define organizational success in relatively clear terms, then monitor their ongoing operations and personnel to determine whether progress is actually being made and, if so, how much? Prior to the advent of the personal or tabletop computer, police field commanders had the luxury of managing according to personal intuition and time-honored past practices. As little strategic planning was taking place, they rarely requested quantitative performance data from their information technology (IT) support departments/divisions. Twenty-five years ago, data were stored and analyzed in large mainframe computers. Even if a field commander recognized the need for timely and accurate data, it could literally take weeks for a data request from the field to be responded to. By that time, circumstances undoubtedly had changed, and the pieces had moved across the chessboard, rendering the requested report or data useless. Policing is a very dynamic business, though, and information is only useful and actionable if it is current and accurate.

Once police field commanders began having personal computers in their own offices, they could easily generate their own reports and maps, as the information was now immediately available to them (and their supervisors!). Data reports quickly began to be produced in house and in real time. Police managers were now able to own, prioritize, and use their own data. Soon these reports were being used by field commanders for decision support, for both short-term tactical decisions and long-term strategic planning. The business of policing had changed dramatically. Forward-thinking police administrators now began to *use* data to leverage resources and guide strategic and tactical decisions.

Today, modern policing has evolved into an evidence-based practice. Performance measurement has become a standard and necessary tool, not simply to account for past actions and decisions, but to inform future decisions and new strategies. As Spence & Keeping (2011) note, "As performance appraisal has evolved in the workplace, we have seen a shift away from focusing on the performance appraisal as an isolated event to viewing it as one part of a larger performance management process" (p. 91). This highlights the important distinction between personal performance appraisal and performance *management*. As opposed to a single measurement that is a "discrete event occurring annually or semi-annually" (p. 85), performance management is "an on-going, systematic approach to improving results through evidence-based decision making, continuous organizational learning, and a focus on accountability for performance" (Mucha, 2011, p. 43). A performance management system "provides feedback to employees on a regular basis so they always know whether or not they're meeting expectations" (Walsh, 2011, p. 15). Some suggest that "the very existence of a rigid, formal review process once a year can actually stifle informal feedback" that would otherwise occur on an on-going basis (Inskeep, 2009). Clearly, an employee's performance should be discussed more than once a year.

Performance management is a progressive new way of doing business that relies upon, "all the concerted actions an organization takes to improve results by applying objective information to management and policy making. … Better information enables elected officials and managers to recognize success, identify problem areas, and respond with appropriate actions—to learn from experience and apply that knowledge to better serve the public" (p. 43). In other words, timely and accurate data should now be routinely used for decision support, to inform and guide decisions before they are actually made (O'Connell & Straub, 2007). Physicians have been using these methods for centuries, utilizing charts, reports, scans, diagnostic tests, and so forth, to plan an appropriate course of action for proper patient care. Police managers are now utilizing similar skills.

Data are now used to help police managers first set long-term strategic goals for the entire organization, then to develop particular tactics to accomplish organizational goals. Performance measurement is therefore not just an administrative exercise that occurs at the end of a year, as a form of bookkeeping or a way of justifying promotions or work already performed. It is a way to continually monitor and guide police work, in its various forms. The organization's mission statement helps administrators establish broad annual goals for the entire agency. Specific division or unit goals are then set directly from that mission, followed by individual performance targets that can then be set for particular officers. This is where the personal performance appraisal process comes in.

## The Need for Individual Performance Appraisal

A police organization can only determine that it is having success if its personnel are accomplishing their assigned tasks in a timely and effective manner. The appraisal of police officers' job performance is therefore a crucial managerial task that equally affects the employee as well as the overall quality of police service (Walsh, 1990). Managerial decisions about officer performance and the quality of police services cannot be made, though, without a logical and objective measurement framework (Roberg, 1979). From an organizational standpoint, it is obviously imperative for a police organization to know exactly what its officers are doing, how much work is being performed, and whether these efforts are having any positive effect. Performance appraisal is also very important to the officers themselves, as appraisal data are often used as the basis for decisions about training, probation, disciplinary action, promotion, merit increases, reductions in force, transfers, and so forth (Holden, 1986). So the critical question is: Does the organization have an effective system in place for personal performance appraisal? Even if it does, a secondary question is whether the system is being used for maximum effectiveness.

The performance evaluation of police personnel becomes even more crucial because the police not only provide public services, but they also fight crime and have the power to significantly restrict rights and freedoms of citizens with their actions or inaction. Any malfeasance or nonfeasance of duty is therefore quite significant. Poor performance by the police can cause immediate harm to individuals and to the community. It should therefore be properly documented and addressed so that corrective actions can be immediately taken. Police are also frequently in public view and are constantly subject to criticism regarding the efficiency and effectiveness of their services (Gaston & King, 1995). It is important to have documentation upon which to rely when responding to citizen complaints and considering the overall quality of an officer's or unit's performance.

The police function represents the most visible and powerful inter-action between a government and its people. If the police perform their role effectively, society benefits immensely. Conversely, with poor police performance, the damage to police confidence and constitutional rights can be irreparable (Travis, 1996). Anecdotal evidence of effectiveness or self-serving statements regarding police productivity is useless in terms of demonstrating progress or justifying the efforts of the police. An objective assessment framework is an absolute necessity.

Police performance appraisal therefore plays a critical role in pro-viding better-quality service to society. Public service agencies, like the police, have an obligation to the citizens they serve to constantly evaluate and improve performance on both the individual and organi-zational levels. A well-designed formal performance appraisal system provides the means to accomplish these goals. In addition, individual performance appraisals give employees feedback about their work and provide supervisors with a reliable, valid instrument on which to base personnel decisions. Performance evaluations are also an ideal way to communicate and reinforce organizational values and positive behav-iors, which will help to increase officer performance and improve ser-vice delivery (Kramer, 1998).

Police job performance evaluation in the work environment is a necessary activity in any police organization (Roberts, 1995). Performance appraisal is critical to the achievement of the mission, goal, and objectives of police departments. Personnel are the arms, legs, and mind of the police service. How all police employees con-tribute in the direction of achieving the overall goals is, to a signifi-cant degree, reflective of how each individual officer performs his or her job. Performance appraisal directly affects both the individual and the agency (Swank & Conser, 1983).

The design, implementation, and continuation of an effective per-formance appraisal system is an important but difficult task faced by the police manager (Fyfe, Greene, & Wilson, 1997). Performance appraisals enable supervisors of police agencies to evaluate the per-formance of their subordinates on a formal and periodic basis and foster a more harmonious working relationship among the mem-bers of the organization (Roberts, 1995). Poorly designed and badly executed performance appraisals can cause a great deal of unnecessary harm.

The identification of a performance problem is not synonymous with the end of one's career. The presumption is that minor deficiencies will be identified early in one's career, documented, monitored, and followed by corrective action, retraining, or enhanced supervision. If there is a problem with a particular employee's work performance, the organization should want to know about it immediately and should be willing and prepared to take the corrective actions necessary to restore the employee in question to adequate performance levels. This is the essence of the notion of employee development.

A well-designed performance appraisal system can be used as a means to shape behavioral responses and smooth the progress of organizational change (Oettmeier & Wycoff, 1999). Officer performance appraisals might also be used to change the service expectations, policing styles, and responsibilities of patrol officers and entire units.

Surprisingly, police organizations have not always evaluated their personnel. During the 1970s, only 80% of American law enforcement agencies were conducting formal evaluations of employees (Geller, 1991). By the 1980s, approximately 80% of the police departments officially appraised their patrol officers at least once a year (Bradley & Pursley, 1987). In the United States today, virtually all police departments now regularly appraise the performance of their officers.

The types of police performance appraisals vary considerably from department to department. Many police departments require quarterly performance appraisals, some perform them annually, some use prepromotional evaluations, and some use a combination. There are unfortunately still some departments that require no performance appraisal or job evaluations at all (Lane, 2010; Templeton, 1995). As we discuss later, this represents an enormous liability risk to the organization, the community, and individual officers.

In addition to those police agencies that do not utilize a performance appraisal system at all, there are many agencies that have a limited or ineffective system in place. Clearly, all performance appraisal systems are obviously not alike. Some are so thoroughly flawed that they are virtually useless. Walsh (1990), in his study of performance appraisal systems that included 150 supervisors from 67 small and medium-sized police departments, revealed that most of the supervisors (93%, N = 114) were using appraisal forms that their departments had merely copied from other police agencies. In one sense, standardization of practice among police agencies in this regard is desirable. But simply "cutting and pasting" another organization's goals, forms, and performance framework is risky business. An effective performance evaluation process must be thoughtfully designed from within (that is, with the active input of various stakeholders throughout the ranks), and performance standards must relate to the particular dynamics and challenges of the community being policed. It must incorporate both community expectations and organizational values.

Today, personal performance data are being utilized for purposes as varied as administrative decisions regarding layoffs, promotions, transfers, grant funding opportunities, compensation and rewards, and employee training and development (Murphy & Cleveland, 1995). Interestingly, in spite of the varied and extensive use of performance appraisal, both organizations and their employees continue to express *dissatisfaction* with the current state of appraisal technology and its application (Banks & Murphy, 1985; Murphy & Cleveland, 1995). It seems that performance appraisal systems are barely able to deliver all of their intended benefits to police organizations. Surveys have revealed widespread discontent in relatively large police departments, which most likely have the resources to obtain the best available appraisal technology (Coutts & Schneider, 2004; Walsh, 1990; Huber, 1983). For example, Coutts and Schneider (2004), in their survey of Canadian police departments, found that most officers were not satisfied with their organization's performance appraisal systems, which were deficient with respect to well-established key components of performance appraisal. The officers also indicated that they had little or no opportunity for input, and received evaluations that were based on personal characteristics (as opposed to performance criteria), and their appraisals did not lead to improved job performance.

In spite of these dissatisfactions, however, managers are typically unwilling to abandon or significantly revise performance appraisal systems, which they still view as a vital tool of management (Meyer, 1991). But police performance appraisal systems are clearly here to stay. They have become an integral part of police administration. The key question going forward is to determine how to intelligently design or modify them to meet the needs of administrators, officers, and their communities. Another important question is how to make raters and the officers they evaluate feel differently about the process. How do we make them understand how important the process actually is?

Performance evaluation systems will almost certainly fail if one or more of the following factors exist:

- Inadequate or unclear job descriptions
- Lack of rater training
- Ambiguity of the rating scale
- Lack of rater buy-in
- Lack of ratee buy-in

There is a lack of research attention about subordinates' reactions to the appraisal process and factors contributing to these reactions (Cardy & Dobbins, 1994; Murphy & Cleveland, 1995). Research has usually focused instead on rating accuracy and rater error (Cardy & Dobbins, 1994). But it seems obvious that even a well-developed and advanced performance appraisal system will fail, if that system is not accepted and supported by employees. It may either be rejected outright, or simply prove itself to be ineffective over time (Carroll & Schneier, 1982; Murphy & Cleveland, 1995). Even a well-designed system will fail without authentic buy-in (Wiersma & Latham, 1986; Tziner, Joanis, & Murphy, 2000; Bernardin & Beatty, 1984). Appraisal systems therefore cannot be imposed upon employees; they should be jointly developed. Employees' attitudes toward performance appraisal may then play an increasingly crucial role in appraisal processes as the systems and procedures continue to develop (Hedge & Borman, 1995).

There is common agreement among performance appraisal researchers that the assessment of employees' reactions to performance appraisals is essential for system acceptance by users and for the efficiency of those evaluations (Keeping & Levy, 2000). Research has clearly demonstrated that a performance appraisal system is not effective unless it probes user satisfaction (Murphy & Cleveland, 1995) and is widely accepted by the users (Latham & Wexley, 1994; Lee, 1985; Landy, Zedeck, & Cleveland, 1983). A nationwide survey of police organizations in the United States indicated that the police departments that provided more training to raters, utilized a variety of performance criteria, and used the performance appraisal for officer development were more satisfied with their evaluation systems than other departments (Lilley & Hinduja, 2007).

It is nearly impossible to obtain an accurate view of a performance review system's effectiveness without soliciting the opinions of those individuals being evaluated. It is crucial to continually learn the reactions and attitudes of both the raters and ratees about the performance appraisal system, since any system ultimately depends on them for its efficiency.

Analyzing the managerial viewpoint is also certainly vital because the effectiveness of a performance appraisal system relies on the manager and his or her capacity to make candid and precise judgments about job performance. It is reasonable to presume that police supervisors would be a suitable source of information about existing police performance appraisal practices (Devries, Morrison, Shullman, & Gerlach, 1986).

Unfortunately, performance appraisal has been an ongoing cause of dissatisfaction and debate both among researchers and practitioners, as there never seems to be a "right" system (Lawler, Mohrman, & Resnik, 1984; Markovich, 1994; Newton & Findlay, 1996). In spite of the high rate of discontent, organizations continue to dedicate much time and resources to performance appraisal, as it is considered a "necessary evil" for human resource management (Roberts, 1995).

In order for the performance evaluation to reach the required target, it is important to critically examine current practices and needs. Once again, this process requires the views and recommendations of both the raters and the ratees about the performance appraisal system (Dobbins, Cardy, & Platz-Vieno, 1990). In a later chapter, we will do just that by exploring two case studies that attempt to measure the opinions of both the raters and ratees of existing police performance appraisal systems in two very diverse locales (Toledo, Ohio, and Ankara, Turkey). The purpose of this inquiry is to determine whether there are any common trends or obvious similarities of opinion. It would certainly be fascinating to identify common professional sentiments that transcend national and cultural boundaries.

Obviously, there are some inherent limitations in attempting to compare the performance evaluation system of the Turkish National Police (TNP) with American police evaluation systems. In Turkey, there is a single uniform system, one national police organization of more than 200,000 officers for the entire country. On the other hand, in the United States, there are virtually as many different evaluation systems as there are police departments in the country. For this reason, we will select and examine the Toledo (Ohio) Police Department's performance evaluation system as a case study, since it allows us to retain the holistic and meaningful characteristics of real-life events, such as managerial and organizational processes (Yin, 2003).

The Toledo Police Department was originally recommended to the authors by the Ohio Association of Chiefs of Police (OACP) as having one of the best performance appraisal systems among the police departments in Ohio. This particular performance appraisal system, which was developed with assistance from Michigan State University, is intended to serve as a feedback mechanism for its employees, providing information on individual levels of performance. These evaluations are also intended to help employees improve their personal performance and to assist in their career development (Supervisor's Guide to Performance Evaluation Systems, 2005).

With the globalization of technology and universalization of information, we now need to view criminal justice systems from a global perspective (Fields & Moore, 2005). This comparative perspective will highlight a broad array of practices, while providing a far deeper understanding of the similarities and the differences between the performance appraisal practices in two very different organizations.

## Theoretical Background

Generally speaking, modern policing is carried out in two different forms: *traditional policing* and *community policing*. Community policing became increasingly popular in the United States during the 1990s. The number of police agencies that are reported to have transitioned from traditional law enforcement to community policing rose rapidly from around 50% in 1994 to nearly 80% in 1998 (Oliver, 1998). Virtually every American police department has adopted some community policing policies and practices, in one form or another, since that time. Community policing principles have been found to alter the key role of police officers, from law enforcers to problem solvers who work with citizens to address the quality of life concerns of the community (Trojanowicz, Kappeler, Gaines, & Bucqueroux, 1998).

It is a question of both philosophy and style. When conducting any type of research upon police organizations, a key question is to inquire whether the organization tends more toward the traditional or community policing ends of the spectrum. Another critical question for community policing departments is: Have their personal performance appraisal methods been supplemented or adjusted to accommodate this transition in operational style? Does the appraisal system being used have the capacity to detect and measure the problem-solving and adaptive performance associated with this type of police work?

In this book, we will examine the Turkish National Police as an organization that has the features of the traditional policing philosophy. In contrast, the Toledo Police Department, like most other American police agencies, operates under the principles of community policing. We will compare and contrast the performance appraisal systems of both departments. One would logically expect these two very distinct police departments with distinct policing styles to require different methods of appraising personal performance.

According to traditional organizational theory, organizations can be described as closed systems that are bureaucratic, mechanistic, and stable (Swanson, Territo, & Taylor, 1998). The administrative structure of traditional policing can be explained through Weber's theory of bureaucracy. According to Weber, two of the most important characteristics of bureaucracy are: (1) the principles of hierarchy and (2) a division of labor that results in specialization. Thus, the organizational structure of traditional policing can be characterized as a bureaucratic, centralized, hierarchical, specialized, and closed organization (Ritzer, 2000).

According to Etzioni, all units in a *bureaucracy* "are coordinated by a set of rules and orders" (as cited in Aydin, 1997, p. 49), and these regulations provide standardization within the organization. Standardization occurs through the use of paper-based or electronic documentation for all of an organization's work. Police organizations represent the quintessential bureaucracy (Guyot, 1979). This results in a rigidly designed organizational structure that causes difficulties in terms of the adaptation of new approaches to the organization.

Traditional police organizations are managed according to the principles of *hierarchy*, which "requires that each lower level of an organization be supervised by a higher level" (Swanson et al., 1998,

p. 158). Accordingly, there is a hierarchical structure in all police organizations, which consists of several rank levels and the use of disciplinary work resulting from this structure. A hierarchical structure has a significant effect upon the operations of an organization. A primary effect is that communication between the ranks is top to bottom. Bosses tell subordinates what they need to know and to do. It rarely works the other way, as upward communication is typically quite limited. Another aspect is the inflexibility that is often caused by a hierarchy. Within every level of rank, duties are defined by clear rules, and although this provides standardization within police organizations, it also significantly limits the decision-making ability of individuals within the organization.

One of the most important principles of Weber's bureaucracy is that division of labor results in *specialization* within organizations. In large organizations, specialization provides effective service and efficiency. On the other hand, it makes organizations very complex in terms of communication and coordination. Specialization also has several advantages, including having well-trained personnel, increased proficiency, and the ability to carry out effective special operations. However, increased specialization may also result in too many internal rules (i.e., red tape) and increased administrative relations within departments. Oftentimes, it decreases overall job performance. Particular tasks, such as criminal investigation, traffic control, narcotics enforcement, and combating terrorism, are typically assigned to specialized units in large police organizations. These units can eventually become "overspecialized." They can become so removed from regular or routine police work that they experience mission drift and fail to either act or consider themselves as typical police officers. Issues of communication, command, and control can also quickly become problematic in very complex and large police organizations (Ritzer, 2000).

The increased bureaucratization of police organizations results in extreme *centralization* and rationalization (Aydin, 1997). In centralized organizations, the top of the hierarchy tends to keep all decision-making power in its hands. Thus, in large police organizations (like the Turkish National Police Department), administrators tend to retain all or most decision-making authority. According to traditional organizational theory, organizations such as these are characterized as *closed systems* where everything is rational, predictable, and certain

(Swanson et al., 1998). Since everything is predictable, traditional bureaucratic organizations consider little need to communicate with their environments. As a result, communication between the community and police organizations is limited. Senior police officials need not consult the community, or their subordinates, as it is assumed that management already knows all that should be known. This is an extremely shortsighted mindset that fails to recognize how dynamic the business of policing actually is.

After some serious and critical questioning of traditional policing, and after decades of civil unrest and rising crime rates, community policing appeared in the United States. By the late 1980s, many police departments in the United States had begun to implement community policing. This movement received a push through the work of Osborne and Gaebler (1993) on "reinventing government." They argued that government had become distant, ineffective, and inefficient. To improve services and regain the public's trust, government, in their view, needed to be restructured to make it more responsive to the citizenry. An important component of their reform plan was *decentralization*. To them, decentralized institutions are more innovative, effective, and responsive, as they are naturally more attuned to citizen concerns than rigidly bureaucratic police organizations.

As the role and mission of the police has shifted from crime fighting to order maintenance and enrichment of the quality of life in our communities, the evaluation of the quality of police service has become vital because police provide services that most citizens cannot obtain elsewhere (Lipsky, 2003).

The basis of the community policing philosophy is that police departments cannot implement crime prevention strategies without cooperating with the community. Community policing emphasizes proactive, open, dynamic, and problem-oriented policing in contrast to the reactive, closed, and incident-driven characteristics of traditional policing (Swanson et al., 1998).

According to Skolnick (1998), community policing has four main principles. The first principle is that problem-oriented policing involves four steps: scanning, analysis, response, and assessment (SARA). Problem-oriented policing can also be implemented without community policing. The second is that better communication between police officers and the community is facilitated by decentralization, rather than a top-down organizational structure. The third is that community policing necessitates citizen involvement. Policing is viewed as a joint enterprise, a partnership. If community members view the police as merely an army of occupation, they are less likely to cooperate with them. Finally, in order to cooperate with each other, police and society should set up neighborhood level organizations.

In general, community policing relies on organizational decentralization and reorientation of patrol resources to facilitate two-way communication between police and the public (Goldstein, 1990). Police are assigned to a permanent beat or area in order to become familiar with the people they serve. Rather than limiting the police mission to crime control and the apprehension of criminals, quality of life and reduction of fear are included as important and measureable goals. Preventing crime, rather than reacting to crime, is emphasized. To accomplish this, reliance is placed upon the development of positive working partnerships between the police and the community in combating crime and disorder (Sparrow, 1988).

While funding opportunities for these types of programs have diminished in the United States in recent years, community policing remains a dominant philosophy both in the United States and abroad. Unlike traditional policing, today's philosophy focuses on providing services that are responsive to the community. Organizationally, bureaucracy and red tape are reduced and operational decision making is lowered to the workforce (or field command) level. The police establish networks of contacts with people representing all walks of life throughout their neighborhoods (Trojanowicz & Bucqueroux, 1990).

Community policing necessitates a fundamental shift in the regulations and tasks of the police. Police are no longer just crime fighters; now police are also problem solvers. Arrest statistics are not dispositive. Perhaps an organization's best officer is one who does not need to make an arrest, but rather uses superior problem-solving and communication skills to prevent an offense from ever occurring.

In a community policing framework, performance appraisals do far more than assess police behavior. They serve as critical vehicles for increasing awareness and understanding, conveying organizational expectations, and rewarding behavior concordant with the broadened police role inherent in community policing. In this way, changing police performance measures may well be vital to the success of community policing (Chandek, 2000).

As police agencies developed from the traditional model of policing toward a strategy of community and problem-oriented policing, it became obvious that the traditional measures of police performance had become outdated and needed to be altered. Performance measurement systems based on clearance rates, numbers of arrests, and response times suggest little in the assessment of police efforts to address community desires and problems. It is certainly desirable for a police department to reduce its overall response times to calls for police service, but what exactly are they doing when they get there? Are they having any effect, making a difference? Police administrators need to consider what outcomes (rather than mere outputs) they desire and must be able to accurately measure and report them. Community concerns clearly need to be addressed while developing police performance appraisal systems (Moore & Braga, 2003).

A key to community-oriented policing is a "systematic approach to policing with the paradigm of instilling and fostering a sense of community ... to improve the quality of life" (Oliver, 1998, p. 51). According to the community policing research conducted by Oettmeier and Wycoff (1999), the advent of community-oriented policing has indicated the need for evaluations to be used to convey and reinforce communication to police officers relating to the mission and values of the department, to document problems in the community, and identify departmental problems that hinder officers from accomplishing their goals. Not surprisingly, a nationwide survey of 600 police organizations in the United States indicated that overall satisfaction with police officer performance appraisal systems was significantly higher among agencies with greater levels of community policing implementation (Lilley & Hinduja, 2006).

This book will closely examine the performance appraisal systems of two very different organizations, the TNP, located in Ankara, Turkey (very traditional and centralized), and the Toledo, Ohio, Police Department (a decentralized, community policing model). Since the law enforcement approaches and the organizational structures of these police organizations are very different, one would expect to see different outcomes in each department in terms of officers' satisfaction of the performance appraisal systems. Performance appraisal systems need to be crafted to fit the organizational systems that they are part of. If organizational systems are different, then the performance appraisal systems they use are also likely to be different. But alterations to personnel appraisal systems do not come easy, particularly within police organizations. Any change in the performance evaluation system will most likely require a change in the overall system of the organization. It is naïve to suggest that a police organization could simply adopt another's performance appraisal system, without making significant modifications to accommodate that department's particular history, culture, personnel, and practices. It is mainly for this reason that many police organizations throughout the world forego radical change, choosing instead to maintain the status quo by tolerating inadequate appraisal systems.

### Purpose of the Book

This book will closely examine the performance appraisal systems of the Ankara and Toledo Police Departments to compare the two systems and identify certain generic, best practices in police performance appraisal that can help improve the system of any modern police organization. We will examine two studies, one conducted in the Ankara Police Department in 2001 and one conducted in the Toledo Police Department during 2006. The purpose is to understand whether there are differences in the practices being employed, as well as the perceptions of the individuals actually appraising performance and being appraised. Such a comparative view also allows us to differentiate universal policing performance traits or practices from those that are culturally specific. Also, a comparison of traditional and community policing philosophies in these two organizations may help us explain how different organizational structures influence officers' attitudes toward the performance appraisal systems.

We will explore whether the appraisal system (traditional vs. modern) matters in terms of affecting the officers' satisfaction with the performance appraisal system in their departments. Are field and command officers' perceptions of the performance evaluation instruments in their departments similar, or do they differ from those of their subordinates? In addition, the nature of the relationship between the officer's perception of the appraisal system and the officer's rank is examined while controlling for the officer's level of education, gender, age, and years of service.

We will employ both qualitative and quantitative methodologies. We would hope that information obtained from this study may also contribute to nationwide assessments of evaluation practices and standards in both countries, and perhaps internationally.

**Organization of the Book**

Chapter 2 presents an overview of police performance appraisal. It begins with the definition, history, purpose, and methods of appraisal along with the sources of appraisal, and the frequency of appraisal. It also examines common errors that police organizations and administrators make when planning and conducting performance appraisals.

Chapter 3 outlines the elements of an effective police performance appraisal system that have emerged from the literature and that will be used as a template to compare and evaluate different appraisal systems. Most importantly, it describes why police performance appraisals typically fail. It also broadly explains core competencies for police officers, the evaluation of supervisors and officers assigned to special units, the postevaluation meeting, and legal issues related to performance appraisal.

Chapter 4 provides general information about the organizational structures of the Turkish National Police and the American police. Then it examines and compares the performance appraisal systems in Ankara and Toledo Police Departments with the best practices depicted in the literature. Chapter 5 examines the officers' attitudes toward the performance appraisal system in the Ankara and Toledo Police Departments. It explores whether there is a relationship between an officer's rank, level of education, gender, years of service, age, and his or her perceptions of the evaluation system. This chapter presents the research design, describes the development of the survey instrument, presents the hypotheses to be tested, and reports the findings of the analyses of the survey. Chapter 6 serves as the conclusion and includes the discussion of the findings and their implications for policy making.

# References

Allen, D. N., & Mayfield, M. G. (1983). Judging police performance. In R. R. Bennet (Ed.), *Police at work: Policy issues and analysis*. Beverly Hills, CA: Sage, 65–86.

Aydin, A. H. (1997). *Police organization and legitimacy*. Aldershot, England: AveburyAshgate Publishing Ltd.

Banks, C. G., & Murphy, K. R. (1985). Toward narrowing the research practice gap in performance appraisal. *Personnel Psychology, 38*(2), 335–345.

Bernardin, H. J., & Beatty, R. W. (1984). *Performance appraisal: Assessing human behavior at work*. Boston, MA: Kent Publishing Company.

Bradley, D., & Pursley, R. (1987). Behaviorally anchored rating scale for patrol officer performance appraisal: Development and evaluation. *Journal of Police Science and Administration, 15*, 37–45.

Cardy, R. L., & Dobbins, G. H. (1994). *Performance appraisal: Alternative perspectives*. Cincinnati, OH: South-Western.

Carroll, S. J., & Schneier, C. E. (1982). *Performance appraisal and review systems: The identification of measurement, and development of performance in organizations*. Glenview, IL: Scott, Foresman.

Catano, V. M., Darr, W., & Campbell, C. A. (2007). Performance appraisal of behavior-based competencies: A reliable and valid procedure. *Personnel Psychology, 60*(1), 201–230.

Chandek, M. S. (2000, Spring). Meaningful and effective performance evaluations in a time of community policing. *Journal of Community Policing, 2*(1).

Coutts, L. M., & Schneider, F. W. (2004). Police officer performance appraisal systems: How good are they? *Policing: An International Journal of Police Strategies and Management, 27*(1), 67–81.

Devries, D., Morrison, A. M., Shullman, S. L., & Gerlach, M. L. (1986). *Performance appraisal on the line*. Greensboro, NC: Center for Creative Leadership.

Dobbins, G. H., Cardy, R. L., & Platz-Vieno, S. J. (1990). A contingency approach to appraisal satisfaction: An initial investigation of the joint effects of organizational variables and appraisal characteristics. *Journal of Management, 16*(3), 619–632.

Fields, C. B., & Moore, R. H. (2005). Comparative criminal justice: Why study? In *Comparative criminal justice: Traditional and nontraditional systems of law and control*. IL: Waveland Press, 3–18.

Fyfe, J. J., Greene, J. R., & Wilson, O. W. (1997). *Police administration*. New York, NY: McGraw-Hill Companies.

Gaston, K. C., & King, L. (1995). Management development and training in the police: A survey of the promotion process. *Journal of European Industrial Training, 19*(7), 20–33.

Geller, W. A. (Ed.). (1991). *Local government police management* (3rd ed.). Washington, DC: International City Management Association.

Goldstein, H. (1990). *Problem-oriented policing*. New York, NY: McGraw-Hill.

Guyot, D. (1979). Bending granite: Attempts to change the rank structure of American police departments. *Journal of Police Science and Administration*, 7(3), 253–284.

Hedge, J. W., & Borman, W. C. (1995). Changing conceptions and practices in performance appraisal. In A. Howard (Ed.), *The changing nature of work* (pp. 451–481). San Francisco, CA: Jossey-Bass.

Holden, R. N. (1986). *Modern police management.* Englewood Cliffs, NJ: Prentice-Hall.

Huber, V. L. (1983). An analysis of performance appraisal practices in the public sector: A review and recommendations. *Public Personnel Management Journal, 12*, 258–267.

Jones, M. (2008). A complexity science view of modern police administration. *Public Administration Quarterly, 32*(3), 433–457.

Kane, J. S., Bernardin, H. H., & Wiatrowski, M. (1995). Performance appraisal. In N. Brewer & C. Wilson (Eds.), *Psychology and policing.* Hillsdale, NJ: Lawrence Erlbaum Associates Publishers.

Keeping, L. M., & Levy, P. E. (2000). Performance appraisal reactions: Measurement, modeling, and method bias. *Journal of Applied Psychology, 85*(5), 708–723.

Kramer, M. (1998). Designing an individualized performance evaluation system. *The FBI Law Enforcement Bulletin, 66,* 20–27.

Krug, J. (1998). Improving the performance appraisal process. *Journal of Management in Engineering, 14*(5), 19–20.

Landy, F., Zedeck, S., & Cleveland, J. (1983). *Performance measurement and theory.* Hillsdale, NJ: Lawrence Erlbaum Associates.

Lane, E. (2010). City discovers evaluations of police, fire not being made as required by law. *The Natchez Democrat,* December 1.

Latham, G. P., & Wexley, K. N. (1994). *Increasing productivity through performance appraisal.* Reading, MA: Addison-Wesley.

Lawler, E. E., Mohrman, Jr., A. M., & Resnik, S. M. (1984). Performance appraisal revisited. *Organizational Dynamics, 13*(1), 20–35.

Lee, C. (1985). Increasing performance appraisal effectiveness. *Academy of Management Review, 10,* 322–332.

Lilley, D., & Hinduja, S. (2006). Officer evaluation in the community policing context. *Policing: An International Journal of Police Strategies and Management, 29*(1), 19–37.

Lilley, D., & Hinduja, S. (2007). Police officer performance appraisal and overall satisfaction. *Journal of Criminal Justice, 35,* 137–150.

Lipsky, M. (2003). Street-level bureaucracy: Dilemmas of the individual in public services. In M. J. Handel (Ed.), *Sociology of organizations: Classic, contemporary and critical readings.* Thousand Oaks, CA: Sage Publications.

Markovich, M. (1994). We can make performance appraisals work. *Compensation and Benefits Review, 26*(3), 25–29.

Meyer, H. (1991). A solution to the performance appraisal feedback enigma. *Academy of Management Executive, 5,* 68–76.

Moore, M. H., & Braga, A. A. (2003). Measuring and improving police performance: The lessons of Compstat and its progeny. *Policing: An International Journal of Police Strategies and Management, 26*(3).

Murphy, K. R., & Cleveland, J. N. (1995). *Understanding performance appraisal: Social, organizational, and goal-oriented perspectives.* Newbury Park, CA: Sage.

Newton, T., & Findlay, P. (1996). Playing God: The performance of appraisal. *Human Resource Management Journal, 6*(3), 42–58.

O'Connell, P. E., & Straub F. (2007). *Performance-based management for police organizations.* Long Grove, IL: Waveland Press.

Oettmeier, T. N., & Wycoff, M. A. (1999). Personnel performance evaluations in the community policing context. In D. J. Kenney and R. P. McNamara (Eds.), *Police and policing: Contemporary issues* (2nd ed.). Westport, CT: Praeger Publishers.

Oliver, W. M. (1998). *Community-oriented policing: A systematic approach to policing.* Upper Saddle River, NJ: Prentice Hall.

Osborne, D., & Gaebler, T. (1993). *Reinventing government: How the entrepreneurial spirit is transforming the public sector.* Reading, MA: Addison-Wesley Pub.

Ritzer, G. (2000). *Classical sociological theory* (5th ed.). New York, NY: McGraw-Hill Companies.

Roberg, R. R. (1979). *Police management and organizational behavior: A contingency approach.* St. Paul, MN: West.

Roberts, L. J. (1995). Performance appraisals in reverse (police agencies). *The FBI Law Enforcement Bulletin, 64*(9), 21–26.

Skolnick, J. H. (1998). Community policing: Chicago style. *Contemporary Sociology—A Journal of Reviews, 24*(5), 527–528.

Sparrow, M. K. (1988). Implementing community policing. In W. M. Oliver (Ed.), *Community policing: Classical readings* (pp. 172–183). Upper Saddle River, NJ: Prentice Hall.

*Supervisor's guide to performance evaluation systems.* (2005). Toledo Police Department, Ohio.

Swank, C. J., & Conser, J. A. (1983). *The police personnel system.* New York, NY: John Wiley & Sons.

Swanson, C. R., Territo, L., & Taylor, R. W. (1998). *Police administration: Structure, processes, and behavior* (4th ed.). Upper Saddle River, NJ: Prentice-Hall.

Templeton, R. E. (1995). Police evaluations: The art of constructive criticism and eloquent praise. *Journal of California Law Enforcement, 29,* 39–41.

Trojanowicz, R., Kappeler, V., Gaines, L., & Bucqueroux, B. (1998). *Community policing: A contemporary perspective* (2nd ed.). Cincinnati, OH: Anderson Publishing.

Trojanowicz, R., & Bucqueroux, B. (1990). *Community policing: A contemporary perspective* (2nd ed.). Cincinnati, OH: Anderson Publishing Co.

Travis, J. (1996). *Measuring what matters, part one: Measures of crime, fear and disorder.* Washington, DC: National Institute of Research in Action, U.S. Department of Justice.

Tziner, A., Joanis, C., & Murphy, K. R. (2000). A comparison of three methods of performance appraisal with regard to goal properties, goal perception and ratee satisfaction. *Group and Organization Management, 25*(2), 175–190.

Walsh, W. F. (1990). Performance evaluation in small and medium police departments: A supervisory perspective. *American Journal of Police, 9,* 93–109.

Wiersma, U., & Latham, G. P. (1986). The practicality of behavioral observation scales and trait scales. *Personnel Psychology, 39*(3), 619–628.

Wolfer, L., & Baker, T. E. (2000). Evaluating small town policing: Methodological issues. *Journal of Police and Criminal Psychology, 15,* 52–63.

Yin, R. (2003). *Case study research: Design and methods* (3rd ed.). Beverly Hills, CA: Sage Publications.

# 2
# Appraising the Performance of Police Officers

## Introduction

This chapter will provide an overview of performance appraisals: the definition, history, purpose, methods, sources, and frequency of performance appraisal. It will also examine common errors that police organizations and administrators make when planning and conducting performance appraisals.

## Definition of the Performance Appraisal

It seems clear that all private and public organizations must utilize a formal or informal appraisal system to measure employee performance. In order for any public agency to answer the question "How are we doing?" as an organization, it is necessary to gather information, to truly reflect, and to determine how individual employees are performing with regard to assigned tasks and unit goals. Performance appraisal is therefore a required process in which, for a specified period of time, an employee's work behaviors or characteristics are individually rated, judged, or described by a rater. The results are not simply kept, but *used* by the organization. Performance appraisal systems are also used as a tool for organizations to motivate their employees to improve performance and productivity (Coens & Jenkins, 2000; Cardy & Dobbins, 1994; Murphy & Cleveland, 1991). Carroll and Schneier (1982) describe performance appraisal as a process of identifying, observing, measuring, and actually *developing* human performance in organizations.

Performance appraisal can generally be defined as the "periodic, formal summary of an employee's job performance that is usually conducted by the immediate superior using some type of standardized rating form" (McGregor, 1960, p. 78). A well-designed performance appraisal system allows the organization to identify, monitor, and record the behavioral characteristics that equate with job performance.

A variety of components or steps are included in the personnel performance appraisal process. Landy and Farr (1980) presented a model of performance appraisal that included these interacting factors: position characteristics, organization characteristics, the purpose of the rating, the rating process, scale development, the rating instrument, rater and ratee characteristics, the observation and storage of performance data, the retrieval and judgment of that performance, analysis of this information, performance description, and in the end, personnel action. Similarly, Mohrman, Resnick-West, and Lawler (1989) identified four important activities in the performance appraisal cycle within organizations: (1) defining what performance is or should be, (2) measuring and evaluating performance, (3) feeding information about that performance back to the individual, and (4) providing information to other organizational systems that use it. Latham and Wexley (1994) listed similar components, but added a review of legal requirements, development of an appraisal instrument, selection and training of observers, and praise or reward for performance.

Regardless of the definition or the specific components included in the process, performance appraisal in most organizations is formal, structured, and mandated. The process generally consists of an interview between the rater (supervisor) and the rate (employee) as well as some type of formal performance documentation.

### History of the Performance Appraisal

Performance appraisal has evolved over the centuries. The process of formally evaluating the performance of employees has been recorded as far back as the third century A.D. in China (Patten, 1977). In the United States, one of the earliest uses of formal performance appraisal was implemented during the late 1880s, when the federal government designed forms to use in rating personal characteristics and work habits of civil servants (Murphy & Cleveland, 1991). During the next several decades, local government agencies and educational institutions began to incorporate various graphic rating scales

(DeNisi, 1996). After World War I, employee performance evaluation systems came into use in private industry. By the early 1950s, they were an accepted practice in many organizations (Devries, Morrison, Shullman, & Gerlach, 1986). By the 1960s, one study indicated that 61% of all public and private organizations used some type of performance appraisal (Murphy & Cleveland, 1991).

The use of formal performance appraisal systems by police administrators is a relatively new phenomenon, originating in the 1960s. O. W. Wilson (1963), perhaps the most influential police leader of that period, claimed that the appraisal of police officers was necessary, but extremely difficult. In their 1973 synthesis of the practices in police performance evaluation, Epstein and Laymon noted that there was a wide diversity of performance appraisal and prediction procedures within police departments. Today, police department performance evaluation procedures still vary widely in complexity, comprehensiveness, and accuracy (Swank & Conser, 1983; Whisenand & Rush, 1998).

### Purpose of the Performance Appraisal

Eichel and Bender (1984) state that performance appraisals are used to evaluate an employee's work performance over a certain time period and to provide feedback and development. Latham and Wexley (1994) largely agreed that performance appraisals should serve only as a summary of feedback and goal setting on a regular basis. Managers conducting performance appraisals must therefore be aware of the employee's job goals and objectives (Landy & Farr, 1980). Managers must also have the opportunity to frequently observe the employee on the job. This helps managers determine whether the observed behavior is satisfactory (in terms of stated rules and goals) and how it compares to the performance of other employees.

Experts and researchers have recommended two extensive uses of performance appraisal in organizations. First, it serves an *administrative purpose* in areas such as reward allocation (salary increases, bonuses) and assignment decisions (transfers, promotions, demotions). Second, it contributes to *employee development* in that it makes possible the identification of their strengths and weaknesses, provides performance feedback, and facilitates exchanges with managers

(Dorfman, Stephan, & Loveland, 1986; Murphy & Cleveland, 1995; NPIA, 2011).

Performance appraisals are commonly used for performance feedback, recognizing individual performance, evaluating the achievement of goals at the organizational level, and identifying individual strengths and weaknesses and poor performance. In addition, it was more widely used to determine salaries, promotion, and redundancies in private sector than in public sector organizations (Abu-Doleh & Weir, 2007).

There are several obvious reasons for evaluations of police employees. First, police department supervisors need information for administrative decisions like promotions, training needs, salary increases, retention, and terminations. Second, police managers need information to give feedback to their officers for career planning and to improve officer motivation (Geller, 1991). Finally, police agencies need training programs, validated selection processes, and officer performance improvement guides. Supervisors should remember that the main purpose of performance appraisal is to improve officer performance (Anderson, 1994). Performance feedback is the key element in a successful performance appraisal.

The research literature is scarce in terms of studies that have examined the types of performance appraisal systems currently in place, specifically the uses of appraisal information within police agencies. In a 1978 survey of police departments in the United States, researchers asked police departments to identify the importance of performance appraisal information for a variety of staffing decisions. The following indicates the portion of police agencies reporting that performance appraisal information was important for each type of decision: dismissal, 90.7%; discipline, 4.4%; assignment/transfer, 81.8%; counseling, 81.8%; training, 75.1%; promotion, 73.5%; and salary increase, 30.3% (Greisinger, Slovak, & Molkup, 1978). Obviously, police administrators were convinced by 1978 that performance appraisals played a critical role in the overall management of their departments.

A 1979 survey of 46 police departments revealed that, although 89% gathered performance information in the form of supervisory ratings, only 34% used this appraisal information as input into personnel decisions. In addition, only 42% used rating information as a source of feedback for counseling or coaching purposes (Lee, Malone,

& Greco, 1981). A content analysis of 1,474 individual rating items on 150 police officer performance appraisal instruments from agencies across the United States indicated that the vast majority of performance rating criteria were oriented toward employee control or limiting mistakes (Lilley & Hinduja, 2006).

Despite the fact that police administrators recognized a need for performance appraisals, few departments were conducting and using them effectively.

## Performance Appraisal Methods

Police performance appraisal systems vary widely in complexity, accuracy, comprehensiveness, and prediction procedures (Walsh & Donovan, 1990). There are three general types of appraisal methods used by police agencies: personal characteristics based, behavior based, and goal based (Hughes, 1990). Let's examine each one of them.

### Personal Characteristics Based

Appraisals that rate personal characteristics of police officers typically rely on a generic numbering process known as Graphic Rating Scales (GRS) to evaluate each area (Whisenand & Rush, 1998). Indeed, the GRS has been the most universally used evaluation method. Although there are several types of scales, the most common one lists factors in one column (i.e., judgment, honesty, confidentiality) and requires raters to place a mark at a point of value. In this method, each personal and professional quality that is thought to be necessary for the successful performance of an employee's job is listed on the rating form to allow supervisors to grade individual factors and tabulate a total grade (Bopp & Whisenand, 1980). This obviously begs the questions: Who decides which qualities are desirable? What are these decisions based upon? While the identification of "professional" qualities appears to be rather straightforward, identification of "personal" qualities seems more nebulous. In 1987, the Michigan State Police conducted a survey of 300 American police departments that revealed that approximately 70% used some form of personal characteristics-based system to evaluate officers (Hughes, 1990). As stated previously, a large percentage of agencies during that time were using no system at all.

Unfortunately, personal characteristics-based performance ratings have no support in the current literature. Jones (1998) referred to characteristic ratings as personality ratings and stated an employee's performance rating defines who they are rather than the quality of work they accomplish. Systems of this type rate attitudes and dispositions rather than actual work performance. Thus, an employee with a cheerful attitude who always seems to be busy will receive a positive appraisal despite the actual level of work performed. This can obviously cause dissent among the rank and file, not only compromising the integrity of the appraisal system, but also undermining morale and the overall productivity of the organization. Personal characteristic ratings, which are also referred to as trait based, have two additional problems: They cannot be improved upon and are often very poorly defined (Wexley & Yukl, 1984). Characteristic ratings are also far more likely to be rejected by the courts (Latham & Wexley, 1994). This fact alone should make police administrators question their continued use. By their very nature, they are more prone to be arbitrary and capricious. Such a system can quickly devolve into a popularity contest, or be so vague or inconsistent as to be totally useless.

For example, leadership may be rated from 1 through 10. However, the rater often does not receive a definition for the term *leadership*. The rater then needs to rely upon his or her personal understanding and experience with this personal quality. Obviously, the standards can and will differ for each rater. Characteristic-based systems are among the oldest and most pervasive types of appraisal used in all types of organizations (Murphy & Cleveland, 1991). Not surprisingly, both officers and administrators have expressed serious reliability and validity concerns regarding this approach because of its inherent subjectivity (Brewer & Wilson, 1995).

*Behaviorally Based*

Another common type of rating instrument attempts to measure employee behavior. In an effort to address validity concerns that have plagued performance appraisals in the past, some police agencies have begun using evaluations that define the specific criteria that are to be assessed and use a standard scale of measure for each officer (Oettmeier & Wycoff, 1997). In this approach, the Behaviorally Anchored Rating Scale (BARS) is often used. The BARS approach lists several behaviors together in categories that range from poor to excellent (Tziner, Kopelman, & Joanis, 1997).

When performance ratings first began to be implemented nationwide, the opinion of many management experts was that only job-specific behaviors should be subject to evaluation. As the use of formal performance ratings increased after the professional era, many police agencies adopted this practice and limited the evaluation of behaviors to aspects that were specific to the job of patrol officers (Epstein & Laymon, 1973). Accordingly, since the primary traditional element of patrol work has been law enforcement, many formal evaluations have focused on behaviors relating to the number of enforcement actions those officers performed (Epstein & Laymon, 1973; Iannone, 1994). As the patrol function has continued to evolve, particularly during the community policing era, our performance appraisal systems have unfortunately failed to keep pace. Patrol supervisors have found it particularly difficult to accurately gauge work that does not produce measureable results (such as the development of personal relationships with community members).

Organizational psychologists have argued that the performance domain generally should be expanded to include other behaviors that are important to the mission and goals of the organization but are not specific to any one job (Motowidlo & Van Scotter, 1994). In other words, we should not be evaluating an employee's performance in a vacuum. We should view it in the context of the overall performance of the unit, division, and entire organization.

This has traditionally been a problem when managing police organizations. Personnel evaluations were generally viewed as a necessary, albeit unsavory task, that was *unrelated* to the performance or strategic direction of the entire agency. Once they were completed, they were rarely if ever consulted again (except as part of the internal promotion or discipline process). As Chiodo suggests, an individual's work objectives must be clearly linked to the organization's goals "through [ ] departmental and teamwork plans" (p. 29). They must be understood as a vital part of the organization's overall sense and respond capabilities. All organizations need to know exactly what their people are doing and how their labors are contributing to the group effort.

To this end, in the United States, the Federal Labor Management Council recently issued a report that recommends a plan for "align[ing] employee performance with agency performance" (Lunney, 2011, p. 1). The work group that prepared this report noted that:

> People working hard to improve the performance of our agencies and people working hard to improve employee performance are often not communicating with each other, but working on parallel tracks. ... We think this disconnect is part of the reason that good employee performance management has been so elusive. ... We do not have a systems problem—our problems are human ones and they are entrenched in the cultures of our agencies (p. 1).

This problem is obviously not limited to police organizations. Perhaps it is actually more acute in policing, due to the very strong organizational culture of police agencies and their pervasive resistance to change.

The key point here is to "ensure [that] staff are aware of the organization's strategic directions. Do they know what the organization's goals are? This must be communicated in a manner that is clear to all levels of staff" (Lunney, 2011, p. 1). Only then will employees and managers truly understand and appreciate the value of the individual performance appraisal system.

Non-job-specific elements, such as volunteering for overtime, helping coworkers, and performing duties that are not required in the job description, can and should be evaluated under the rubric of contextual performance (Borman & Motowidlo, 1993). Additionally, since the function of police officers is broadened under the community policing concept, managers may increasingly be required to evaluate behaviors, such as problem solving and community outreach, that support organizational efforts and are not limited to job-specific criteria.

This is a central point. Performance appraisals must be designed and implemented in such a way as to measure (or attempt to measure) a ratee's relative level of *'motivation'* and *'engagement'*. These are not merely subjective conclusions made by supervisors. This is a behavioral assessment that is based upon observed facts. *Motivation* is generally defined as "the arousal, direction, intensity and persistence of *voluntary actions that are goal directed.*" (Penney et al., 2011, p. 298). It is therefore essential that a supervisor document all instances where an officer volunteered to perform additional work, or did so quietly on his/her own. Interestingly, in any organization (not just police organizations), motivation levels vary from officer to officer. They also undoubtedly vary throughout the course of one's career.

*Engagement* generally refers to "focused energy that is directed toward organizational goals" (Bakker, 2011, p. 265). Engaged employees are "fully, physically, cognitively, and emotionally connected with their work roles" (p. 265). Engaged workers have also been found to "transfer their engagement to others in their immediate environment" thereby "improve[ing] team performance" (p. 267). Unfortunately, engagement levels also vary widely from employee to employee. Recent studies even suggest that "engagement may also fluctuate within persons from day to day" (p. 266). Despite their variance, both engagement and motivation should be periodically checked. All organizations must ensure that their employees view their work positively, perform eagerly and choose to have a positive impact in the workplace.

Studies have indicated that behaviorally or activity-based methods exhibit a significant improvement in reliability and validity over characteristic-based systems (Tziner et al., 1997). For that reason alone, they should replace attitudinally based systems. In addition, behaviorally based systems get away from measuring subjective personal characteristics and instead measure observable, critical behaviors that are related to specific job dimensions (Bopp & Whisenand, 1980). Such a system is far more likely to withstand legal scrutiny.

The Mixed Standard Rating Scale is another method similar to BARS. Froemel and Furcon (1982) used this method when they created a police officer evaluation process for the Miami, Florida, Police Department. This method bases evaluation upon observed performance stated in behavioral terms, which does not allow for abstract traits or characteristics. This method has been implemented in some organizations in an effort to limit inherent rater bias (Blanz & Ghiselli, 1972). Prien and Hughes (1987), using a state government sample, showed that mixed standard scales can be used to identify and minimize individual rater error and system-wide problems.

However, mixed standard rating scales have been criticized as being too complicated. Because the mixed standard scales require raters to be consistent throughout the rating process, conflicting scores are eliminated. Although this method may improve rating consistency, it occasionally results in missing data (Dedrick, Dobbins, & Desselles, 1990).

*Goal Based*

Management by Objectives (MBO) is a goal-based approach that differs from traditional performance appraisal methods (Drucker, 1954). In this approach, employees are evaluated on what they contribute to the goals and objectives of the organization. The process involves defining the mission of the agency, establishing long-term goals, and developing step-by-step objectives (Wanguri, 1995). Obviously, if the organization is at all unclear about its stated mission and goals, such a system of personal performance appraisal will not be feasible. Because management by objectives focuses on goals rather than behaviors, it is subject to the same criticism as former quantitative systems that totaled outputs without addressing human relations. In policing, the process may be as important as the goal. Further, since community policing principles emphasize attributes such as concern for the neighborhood and sensitivity to citizen complaints, rigid goal-based methods have been used less frequently in recent years (Whisenand & Rush, 1998).

An entirely different appraisal approach is offered by D. J. Van Meter. In his text, *Evaluating Dysfunctional Police Performance* (2001), he proposes a "Z base" rating system whereby employees are initially assumed to be quite competent and productive. Such employees receive a score of zero under this system. Van Meter suggests that "it is assumed, unless proven otherwise, that all employees have the desire, opportunity and abilities to perform similar[ly] and they have no uncorrected performance problems." (p. 7) If, on the other hand, an employee has failed to meet standards in some way and performance has resulted in one or more documented deficiencies, an action plan for correction is made and the employee is awarded an opportunity to correct any deficiency. (p. 7) If the deficiency goes uncorrected, this system calculates the time and costs related to this intervention and attempted correction. That figure is added to the employee's initial (neutral) performance score. The employee's final score—the Z score

—would then vary from the standard. Once again, under this system, an employee's score should be as close to zero as possible.

What is so unique about this approach is that the calculated costs of correction are generated by computer. This system therefore does not rely upon a supervisor's rating. It thereby avoids all subjective biases associated with traditional performance appraisals and provides a far more objective information source for making and defending management and employment decisions.

Van Meter's appraisal system has been used by several police departments in the United States and serves as an alternative appraisal paradigm that should be explored by police organizations, whether or not it is ultimately developed or implemented by them.

### Various Sources of Appraisal

There are several sources of performance appraisal, including those conducted by supervisors, peers, self, subordinates, and multiple sources of appraisal. We will examine each of these in detail.

### Supervisory Appraisal

An employee typically receives a performance appraisal from his or her supervisor. This is the most common practice in all organizations (Cleveland, Murphy, & Williams, 1989). This is also the most logical approach to performance appraisal. Supervisors who have sufficient job knowledge and access to the employee should be the raters (Roberts, 1998). Nearly all police agencies that conduct formal evaluations allow the immediate supervisor to rate the officer (Hughes, 1990; Lilley & Hinduja, 2007). However, it is not clear that this is the optimal practice (Kane & Lawler, 1979). A supervisor's appraisal is often lenient because of the desire to avoid conflict with the employee being appraised. Longenecker, Gioia, and Sims (1987) found that conducting appraisals is often a highly emotional process for managers, further reducing objectivity and accuracy. For these reasons, additional sources of performance appraisal may be needed.

Numerous studies have identified conscious *rating distortion* among evaluators (Spence & Keeping, 2011). This phenomenon has been linked directly to the "prevalence of rater inaccuracy and ineffective performance appraisals" (p. 86). Perhaps rater distortion explains (at least partially) the continual frustration among practitioners, who view personnel performance appraisal as somewhat of an elaborate organizational charade that is simply not based upon reality.

Police supervisors are only human. Like other managers, they "have idiosyncrasies, motives, and pressures that influence ratings" (p. 86). In any organization, there is a tendency for managers to be less-than-truthful when conducting these appraisals. As Spence and Keeping (2011) note, "Managers possess a natural reluctance to evaluate the worth of other human beings. ... [M]anagers might have a difficult time switching from acting as inspirers and motivators to judicial evaluators" (p. 87). Supervisors often wish to avoid confrontation and to make themselves look like more effective managers. Raters have been regularly found to "inflate performance ratings due to a perception that other raters inflate their ratings as well" (p. 88). Organizational "politics" is another major concern that has been identified as a significant source of distortion among raters.

The rates themselves can also be less-than-truthful. Research has identified a variety of impression management techniques that are commonly used by employees to influence the evaluation process (see, e.g., Arif, et al., 2011; Spence & Keeping, 2011).

There is another interesting phenomenon that distorts the employee evaluation process. It has been identified as "managerial network influence," a social influence mechanism that exists in many organizations (Castilla, 2011, p. 668). This occurs when managers either formally of informally share opinions about the work of their subordinates. In the field of policing, assessments of employees are often shared, particularly among supervisors who are structurally or socially connected to one another. An "echo" develops, whereby:

> Individuals agree with each other even when such agreement may be illusory. It is possible that when a manager expresses a predisposition toward an employee, third parties select stories and anecdotes consistent with the flow of the conversation, thereby reinforcing the manager's account. ... Performance evaluations can [ ] be amplified toward positive or negative extremes by third-party members of a network. ... Managers' ratings of a given employee are thus not necessarily independent of each other (p. 670).

Supervisors must be made aware of such threats to objectivity and must ensure that each and every employee evaluation is properly prepared and is based upon fact. Failure to do so could not only jeopardize the entire evaluation system but potentially subject both the organization and the individual manager to liability.

*Peer Appraisal*

Coworkers who frequently interact with the person being evaluated can conduct peer appraisal. Peer appraisals have been found to have higher reliability and validity than appraisal from other sources (Kremer, 1990). Love (1981) found peer appraisals to be reliable and valid because reliability is affected positively by daily interactions among peers, and use of peers as raters makes it possible to get a number of independent judgments. Coworkers have ample opportunity to observe an officer's behaviors regarding tactics and safety, motor vehicle operation, the handling of prisoners, and so forth. Love (1981) contended, though, that to be reliable and valid, peer appraisals must be anonymous. Officers will be far less likely to be candid if they fear retribution from a supervisor or coworker of the officer being appraised. Gordon and Medland (1965) found that peer appraisals are reliable even when the person transfers from one group to another within the same organization. Further, appraisals made by peers with a short period of acquaintance have been found to be as good as those made by peers with longer periods of acquaintance (Hollander, 1965). Peers therefore can provide a valuable source of objective input into the performance appraisal process. Peer evaluations have been used in a number of professional settings. Often, peer raters are asked to comment upon actual cases. For example, their attention can be drawn to a particular case or circumstance and they can be asked, "Would most experienced, competent officers have handled the case differently? In all respects?" (see, e.g., Haines, Ammann, Beehrle-Hobbs, & Groppi, 2010). An even more provocative approach is to ask a peer, "Would you wish to regularly work with this officer? Why or why not?" This latter inquiry obviously depends upon the candidness and honesty of the respondents. For this reason, they should be assured that there will be no personal attribution for negative comments.

Some, however, have argued against peer appraisals, stating that the case for peer assessment has not been systematically studied (Brief, 1980). A considerable concern with peer appraisal is that the behaviors observed must be relevant to the performance dimensions being evaluated. This can be addressed by supervisors through the careful development of appraisal questions and forms. Coworker input can still be extremely accurate and valuable as long as coworkers frequently have the opportunity to observe the actual performance dimensions being evaluated.

Another valid concern is how friendship may affect peer appraisal. Performance appraisals are useless in that their scales are artificially inflated by officers wishing to support their friends. First-line supervisors would obviously need to review appraisals and monitor the system for this type of abuse. Interestingly, Mumford (1983) found that peer assessments are only minimally influenced by friendship, race, or gender.

### Self-Appraisal

Self-appraisal is conducted by oneself, the person being evaluated. An effective self-appraisal process includes a thorough job description to remove ambiguity and establish clear objectives to measure against performance (Campbell & Lee, 1988). Meyer (1991) indicated that self-appraisal enhances employee dignity and self-respect and allows the manager to be in a counselor role rather than simply seeming judgmental or punitive. This helps to increase an employee's understanding of organizational, unit, and personal goals, as well as the need for developmental plans. More importantly, self-appraisal motivates the employee and tends to reduce employee defensiveness (Farh, Werbel, & Bedian, 1988; Lane & Herriot, 1990).

It seems likely that one would self-appraise at a higher level than one's actual skill and competency level. This is human nature; we always tend to see ourselves in a positive light. In a meta-analysis of self-appraisal conducted by Mabe and West (1982), concern about people's tendency to overestimate their abilities was found to be unwarranted. Researchers found that telling people that their self-appraisal would be verified against other performance criteria decreased the tendency for them to rate themselves higher, further increasing self-appraisal validity (Farh et al., 1988). Self-appraisals have generally proven to be accurate and useful to administrators. They should therefore be considered in any performance appraisal framework.

## Subordinate Appraisal

Employees who are lower in organizational rank than the person being evaluated conduct subordinate appraisals. Subordinate appraisals are rarely used due to the more commonly used top-down approach and the fear that subordinate appraisal will undermine management (Bernadin & Beatty, 1984). They can, however, provide useful information about the performance of police supervisors, especially during the probationary period or prior to promotion. It is important to note that subordinate appraisal should be conducted only if there are more than four subordinates participating, in order to increase anonymity. Also, subordinate appraisal should be used only as a supplement to manager appraisal, not as a replacement (Whetstone, 1994; Lawler & Mohrman, 1989).

## Multisource Appraisal

Multisource appraisal is defined as employee feedback gathered from a combination of the sources mentioned above. This approach is used widely today in private organizations (London & Smither, 1995). Recent studies have shown that the use of multiple raters significantly increases validity (Whisenand & Rush, 1998). This type of appraisal is often referred to as a 360-degree feedback process that provides an opportunity to receive feedback from individuals above, below, and lateral in the organizational hierarchy, as well as from individuals outside the organization (Dalessio, 1998). The 360-degree approach is growing in popularity in both the private and public sectors and has the distinct advantage of providing feedback from every aspect of the employee's work environment (Wanguri, 1995). The 360-degree appraisal is most useful when everyone participates in the feedback process or when an individual actively seeks personal development (Wimer, 2002). Unfortunately, this method is not used as frequently as it should be within the field of policing. It should be strongly considered for police supervisors (generally not police officers) of every rank.

Proponents of multisource appraisals argue that 360-degree feedback can build more effective work relationships, increase opportunities for employee involvement, resolve conflict, and demonstrate respect for employee opinions on the part of top management (McCarthy & Garavan, 2001; Mabey, 2001). Meanwhile, critics indicate that the 360-degree appraisal was intended for use with employee development, and not as an appraisal technique since bias such as relationships and friendships between people may impair ratings (Garavan, Morley, & Flynn, 1997).

The major drawbacks of this approach are that it is quite time-consuming and typically very costly in comparison with more traditional methods. If the process is not thoughtfully, candidly, or sincerely undertaken, it can easily be undermined (e.g., reciprocal praise, such as "you be kind to me in your evaluation and I will do the same!"). In addition, many officers have expressed concern over the inherent political implications of such a process (Oettmeier & Wycoff, 1997).

With the traditional appraisal approach, the officer only had to focus on pleasing the supervisor. In the 360-degree method, the officer must try to please everybody all of the time. Further, some veteran officers have expressed concern about being evaluated by coworkers that have little job experience (Oettmeier & Wycoff, 1997). However, since community policing emphasizes teamwork and places value in the opinion of citizens, there is some logic in incorporating some form of community feedback into the evaluation process. Moreover, since the use of multiple raters may increase validity, administrators should consider the possibility of employing a balance between extremes with regard to sources of rating information.

Interestingly, there is some research that suggests that group discussion, such as that which takes place during a 360 evaluation, can actually inflate positive impressions and make ratings less accurate (Palmer & Loveland, 2008). Perhaps 360 evaluators should submit their reviews independently, without collaborating with their fellow evaluators, so as to avoid this problem.

As with any new program or police reform effort, agencies should proceed thoughtfully and carefully. Rather than merely adopting and implementing a new policy or program job-wide, a more rational approach is to develop a pilot program and study its effect. Police organizations contemplating use of the 360 evaluation should therefore use it sparingly and study its use before deciding upon widespread implementation. This is a wise course of action that should become standard practice for any police agency considering a new program; particularly one related to personnel matters.

### Frequency of the Performance Appraisal

The concept applied to the frequency of appraisal is time span of discretion. The time span of discretion is defined as the length of time between the point at which a job incumbent is given a task and the point at which below-standard performance could occur (Kane & Lawler, 1979). The frequency of appraisal is a key in appraisal system success (Bernardin & Beatty, 1984). The attributes of the job and the characteristics of employees determine appraisal frequency (Bernardin & Beatty, 1984).

Ideally, police supervisors should document and comment upon the performance of their subordinates on an ongoing basis. This means that periodic notations should regularly be made throughout the year. Unfortunately, that is not always the case. Many supervisors only document aberrant performance, that is, performance that is particularly good or particularly bad. Others do not document behaviors at all, thereby waiting for the formal evaluation period to arrive and unnecessarily complicating the formal evaluation process. These supervisors will experience great difficulty in completing evaluations, as they will have very little substance to rely upon. They will also undoubtedly criticize the entire system. Supervisors will find that frequent documentation is an absolute necessity. Also, notations that describe an officer's *typical* or *usual* performance levels may prove to be far more helpful than merely noting aberrations, and should greatly facilitate the formal evaluation process. Generally speaking, ratees welcome frequent feedback, particularly with regard to observed deficiencies. Ratees prefer to be informed about problems at the time they occur, so that corrective measures can be taken.

Van Maanen (1976) found that new employees required more frequent appraisals than employees with longer tenure. Bernardin and Beatty (1984) recommend conducting performance appraisals more often than every six months and the use of a diary to track employee performance for greater accuracy. Performance review should be an ongoing process, though, rather than an event. In actual practice, the norm in organizations is to conduct performance appraisals annually (Murphy & Cleveland, 1995). Approximately 80% of police agencies formally evaluate patrol officers at least once a year (Bradley & Pursley, 1987). Management experts have suggested that semiannual evaluation may be better than annual ratings in assisting rater recall and feedback to the employee (Brewer & Wilson, 1995).

Due to associated costs, perhaps this could be done only for officers who: (1) are on probation, (2) have recently received a below average evaluation, or (3) recently have been or are about to be promoted.

### Known Problems Associated With Employee Performance Appraisal

No matter how well an appraisal system is designed, certain problems are bound to surface. Human nature dictates that rating errors will occur naturally, not due to any malice or negligence on the part of the raters. These errors occur in all work settings and are certainly not limited to police work. They are generally viewed as being persistent and problematic, as the integrity of the entire evaluation process must be ensured (Latham & Wexley, 1994).

Unfortunately, even if all precautions are taken, "inadvertent judgmental biases seem to be an inherent feature of rating processes and outcomes" (Jacobs & Kozlowski, 1985, p. 201). They cannot be totally eliminated. At best, organizations can recognize their existence, properly train their personnel, and hope to reduce the likelihood that these problems will occur:

#### Halo Effect

Halo effect is "the longest recognized, most pervasive, and yet least understood form of rating error" (Jacobs & Kozlowski, 1985, p. 201). Indeed, it appears to be an inherent part of employee performance appraisal. Halo effect refers to a rater's tendency to rate an employee based on general impression of the rate, rather than rating him or her upon specific observations and different performance dimensions (Pulakos, 1997). For example, a police officer who issues several citations and is rarely complained about by citizens will be rated overall as an excellent employee by the supervisor, even when that officer may in fact be incompetent in other areas, such as dealing with mentally ill suspects and report writing. It is a strong tendency for:

> The rater to think of the person in general as rather good or rather inferior and to color the judgment of the separate qualities by this general feeling. The implication is that an overall impression causes or forces the ratings of separate dimensions to be consistent with a global evaluation, even when the rater has sufficient information to render independent judgments of the dimensions. (Jacobs & Kozlowski, 1985, p. 202)

The point is that each performance dimension and all work-related skills and behaviors (whether good or bad) need to be evaluated independently. Each employee has strong and weak points, but the halo effect tends to erase these differences. Supervisors must be informed about the halo effect as a necessary part of their rater training. They should be directed to support all conclusory statements with specific examples of rate behaviors and skills. The assumption is that proper training, combined with increased observation of performance-relevant rate behavior, will either prevent or substantially reduce the likelihood of halo errors.

On a related issue, research has also disclosed "positive escalation" of performance scores of employees who were initially hired by the evaluator (Slaughter & Greguras, 2008). This could also arguably apply to the evaluation of detectives or officers who are placed on special assignment by the evaluating supervisor. Police agencies should be aware of this phenomenon and should take appropriate steps to ensure objectivity.

*Primacy and Recency Effects*

Primacy effect takes place when the appraised individual's early performance is noted and not the whole observed performance. The recency effect takes place when only the last period is taken into consideration (Bernardin & Beatty, 1984).

*Central Tendency*

This is a tendency for raters to give all employees around the mid-range of performance (Pulakos, 1997). Thus, if a department's rating scale is 5 = outstanding, 4 = exceeds standards, 3 = meets expected standards, 2 = below expected standards, and 1 = unsatisfactory, virtually all rated officers will receive a 3. Central tendency is a particularly significant problem in police evaluations. Police supervisors quickly learn that a particularly favorable evaluation, as well as a particularly poor evaluation, needs to be very well documented. Both instances require a "paper trail" to justify the supervisor's conclusions. This justification takes the form of narrative descriptions of the ratee's performance, vis-à-vis other officers within the unit. The rater must provide a detailed account of how the ratee's performance varies from the mean, and why the rater believes that variance to be significant. In an ever-litigious society, supervisors are loathe to express their true impressions too freely, as they fear being challenged or contradicted by their own supervisors or disgruntled subordinates. It is far easier to rate all subordinates as "average" or "meets standards" and avoid any such second-guessing of their judgments and opinions.

Researchers have also identified *severity* as the tendency for raters to rate everyone with low ratings, and *leniency* as the tendency for all employees to receive high ratings (Pulakos, 1997). Bernardin, Cooke, and Villanova (2000) called leniency endemic to virtually all rating processes and said that it jeopardizes the validity of the rating process. The last error identified is *rater bias* and *characteristics*, where the evaluator's personal characteristics and biases may affect the performance appraisal process (Geller, 1991).

Training has been shown to reduce common errors (Bernardin & Pence, 1980; Bernardin et al., 2000). Training for both raters and ratees on how to complete the performance appraisal process may also result in higher levels of satisfaction and acceptance of the process (Catano, Darr, & Campbell, 2007; Narcisse & Harcourt, 2008). Virtually all organizations should therefore constantly provide training to the raters in order to decrease evaluation errors. Supervisors should obviously have sufficient knowledge and training to properly implement the performance appraisal.

# Conclusion

This chapter provided an overview of performance appraisals and discussed why performance appraisal is an essential part of police work. Performance appraisal is a required process in which, for a specified period of time, an employee's work behaviors or characteristics are individually rated, judged or described by a rater. Performance appraisal systems are also used as a tool for organizations to improve employee performance and motivation.

Unfortunately, for a host of reasons, dissatisfaction with performance appraisal seems to be the norm (Bernardin, Kane, Ross, Spina, & Johnson, 1995; Murphy & Cleveland, 1995). Police officers, supervisors, and policy makers share a common sense of frustration with current performance appraisal methods. Many view the process as being deficient, but consider their own systems as being "the best one available." This raises very important questions: Can these systems be improved upon? To what extent do they vary from identified best practices? What can be learned by comparing existing systems to established best practices? Widespread dissatisfaction raises serious questions about the degree to which police organizations integrate the accepted key mechanisms into their performance appraisal systems. Chapter 3 will present elements of an effective appraisal system.

# References

Abu-Doleh, J., & Weir, D. (2007). Dimensions of performance appraisal systems in Jordanian private and public organizations. *International Journal of Human Resource Management, 18*(1), 75–84.

Anderson, D. (1994). *Performance appraisal: A different approach* (FBI Law Enforcement Bulletin). Washington, DC: FBI.

Bernardin, H. J., & Beatty, R. W. (1984). *Performance appraisal: Assessing human behavior at work.* Boston, MA: Kent Publishing Company.

Bernardin, H. J., Cooke, D. K., & Villanova, P. (2000). Conscientiousness and agreeableness as predictors of rating leniency. *Journal of Applied Psychology, 85*(2), 232–234.

Bernardin, H. J., Kane, J. S., Ross, S., Spina, D. S., & Johnson, D. L. (1995). Performance appraisal design, development, and implementation. In G. R. Ferris, S. D. Rosen, & D. T. Barnum (Eds.), *Handbook of human resource management* (pp. 462–493). Cambridge, MA: Blackwell.

Bernardin, H. J., & Pence, E. C. (1980). Effects of rater training: Creating new response sets and decreasing accuracy. *Journal of Applied Psychology, 65*(1), 60–66.

Blanz, F., & Ghiselli, E. (1972). The mixed standard rating scale: A new rating system. *Personnel Psychology, 25*(2), 185–199.

Bopp, W., & Whisenand, P. (1980). *Police personnel administration* (2nd ed.). Boston, MA: Allyn and Bacon.

Borman, W., & Motowidlo, S. (1993). Expanding the criterion domain to include elements of contextual performance. In N. Schmitt & W. Borman (Eds.), *Personnel selection in organizations* (pp. 71–98). San Francisco, CA: Jossey-Bass.

Bradley, D., & Pursley, R. (1987). Behaviorally anchored rating scale for patrol officer performance appraisal: Development and evaluation. *Journal of Police Science and Administration, 15,* 37–45.

Brewer, N., & Wilson, C. (1995). *Psychology and policing.* Hillsdale, NJ: Lawrence.

Brief, A. P. (1980). How to manage managerial stress. *Personnel, 57*(5), 25–30.

Campbell, D., & Lee, C. (1988). Self-appraisal in performance evaluation: Development versus evaluation. *Academy of Management Review, 13*(2), 302–314.

Cardy, R. L., & Dobbins, G. H. (1994). *Performance appraisal: Alternative perspectives.* Cincinnati, OH: South-Western.

Carroll, S. J., & Schneier, C. E. (1982). *Performance appraisal and review systems: The identification of measurement, and development of performance in organizations.* Glenview, IL: Scott, Foresman.

Catano, V. M., Darr, W., & Campbell, C. A. (2007). Performance appraisal of behavior-based competencies: A reliable and valid procedure. *Personnel Psychology, 60*(1), 201–230.

Cleveland, J. N., Murphy, K. R., & Williams, R. E. (1989). Multiple uses of performance appraisal. *Journal of Applied Psychology, 74*(1), 130–135.

Coens, T., & Jenkins, M. (2000). *Abolishing performance appraisals.* San Francisco, CA: Berrett-Koehler Publishers.

Dalessio, A. T. (1998). Using multisource feedback for employee development and personnel decisions. In J. W. Smither (Ed.), *Performance appraisal: State of the art in practice* (pp. 278–330). San Francisco, CA: Jossey-Bass.

Dedrick, E., Dobbins, G., & Desselles, M. (1990). The accuracy of evaluations made by logical and illogical raters using a mixed standard scale format. *Educational and Psychological Measurement, 50*(2), 411– 412.

DeNisi, A. (1996). *Cognitive approach to performance appraisal: A program of research.* New York, NY: Routledge.

Devries, D., Morrison, A. M., Shullman, S. L., & Gerlach, M. L. (1986). *Performance appraisal on the line.* Greensboro, NC: Center for Creative Leadership.

Dorfman, P. W., Stephan, W. G., & Loveland, J. (1986). Performance appraisal behaviors: Supervisors perceptions and subordinates reactions. *Personnel Psychology, 39*(3), 579–597.

Drucker, P. (1954). *The practice of management.* New York, NY: Harper and Brothers.

Eichel, E., & Bender, H. (1984). *Performance appraisal: A study of current techniques.* New York, NY: American Management Associations.

Epstein, S., & Laymon, R. S. (1973). *Guidelines for police performance appraisal, promotion and placement procedures.* Washington, DC: Law Enforcement Assistance Administration.

Farh, J. L., Werbel, J. D., & Bedian, A. G. (1988). An empirical investigation of self-appraisal-based performance evaluation. *Personnel Psychology, 41*(1), 141–156.

Froemel, E. C., & Furcon, J. (1982). *The development and validation of job performance appraisal procedures for the positions of police officer, sergeant, lieutenant, and captain in the Miami, Florida Police Department.* Chicago, IL: University of Chicago.

Garavan, T., Morley, M., & Flynn, M. (1997). 360 degree feedback: Its role in employee development. *Journal of Management Development, 16*, 134–147.

Geller, W. A. (Ed.). (1991). *Local government police management* (3rd ed.). Washington, DC: International City Management Association.

Gordon, L. V., & Medland, F. F. (1965), Leadership aspiration and leadership ability. *Psychological Reports, 17*, 388–390.

Greisinger, G. W., Slovak J. S., & Molkup, J. J. (1978). *Police personnel practices in forty-two American cities.* Washington, DC: Public Administration Service.

Haines, S. T., Ammann, R. R., Beehrle-Hobbs, D., & Groppi, J. A. (2010). Protected professional practice evaluation: A continuous quality-improvement process. *Journal of Health-System Pharmacy, 67*(22), 1933–1940.

Hollander, E. P. (1965). Validity of peer nominations in predicting a distant performance criterion. *Journal of Applied Psychology, 49*(6), 434–438.

Hughes, F. V. (1990). Performance appraisal systems in law enforcement. Unpublished doctoral dissertation, Michigan State University, Lansing, MI.

Iannone, N. F. (1994). *Supervision of police personnel* (5th ed.). Englewood Cliffs, NJ: Prentice Hall.

Jacobs, R., & Kozlowski, S. W. (1985). A closer look at halo error in performance ratings. *Academy of Management Journal, 28*, 201–212.

Jones, T. L. (1998, July). Developing performance standards. *Law and Order*, 109–112.

Kane, J. S., & Lawler, E. E. (1979). Performance appraisal effectiveness: Its assessment and determinants. In B. Staw (Ed.), *Research in organizational behavior* (Vol. 1, pp. 425–478). Greenwich, CT: JAI Press.

Kremer, J. F. (1990). Construct validity of multiple measures in teaching, research, and service and reliability of peer ratings. *Journal of Educational Psychology, 82*(2), 213–218.

Landy, F. J., & Farr, J. L. (1980). Performance rating. *Psychological Bulletin, 87*(1), 72–107.

Lane, J., & Herriot, P. (1990). Self-ratings, supervisor ratings, positions and performance. *Journal of Occupational Psychology, 63*(1), 77–88.

Latham, G. P., & Wexley, K. N. (1994). *Increasing productivity through performance appraisal.* Reading, MA: Addison-Wesley.

Lawler, E. E., & Mohrman, A. M. (1989). *Designing performance appraisal systems: Aligning appraisals and organizational realities.* Los Angeles, CA: Jossey-Bass.

Lee, R., Malone, M., & Greco, S. (1981). Multitrait-multimethod-multirater analysis of performance ratings for law enforcement personnel. *Journal of Applied Psychology, 66*(5), 625–632.

Lilley, D., & Hinduja, S. (2006). Organizational values and police officer evaluation: A content comparison between traditional and community policing agencies. *Police Quarterly, 9*, 411–439.

Lilley, D., & Hinduja, S. (2007). Police officer performance appraisal and overall satisfaction. *Journal of Criminal Justice, 35*, 137–150.

London, M., & Smither, J. W. (1995). Can multisource feedback change perceptions of goal accomplishment, self-evaluations, and performance-related outcomes? Theory-based applications and directions for research. *Personnel Psychology, 48*(4), 803–839.

Longenecker, C., Gioia, D., & Sims, H. (1987). Behind the mask: The politics of employee appraisal. *Academy of Management Executive, 1*, 183–193.

Love, K. G. (1981). Comparison of peer assessment methods: Reliability, validity, friendship bias, and user reaction. *Journal of Applied Psychology, 66*(4), 451–457.

Mabe, P. M., & West, S. G. (1982). Validity of self-evaluations of ability: A review and meta-analysis. *Journal of Applied Psychology, 67*(3), 280–296.

Mabey, C. (2001). Closing the circle: Participant views of a 360 degree feedback programme. *Human Resource Management Journal, 11*(1), 41–53.

Narcisse, S., & Harcourt, M. (2008). Employee fairness perceptions of performance appraisal: A Saint Lucian case study. *International Journal of Human Resource Management, 19*(6), 1152–1169.

McCarthy, A. M., & Garavan, T. N. (2001). 360 degree feedback processes: Performance improvement and employee career development. *Journal of European Industrial Training, 25*(1), 5–32.

McGregor, D. (1960). *The human side of enterprise.* New York, NY: McGraw-Hill.

Meyer, H. (1991). A solution to the performance appraisal feedback enigma. *Academy of Management Executive, 5*, 68–76.

Mohrman, A. M., Resnick-West, S., & Lawler, E. E. (1989). *Designing performance appraisal systems: Aligning appraisals and organizational realities.* San Francisco, CA: Jossey-Bass.

Motowidlo, S., & Van Scotter, J. (1994). Evidence that task performance should be distinguished from contextual performance. *Journal of Applied Psychology, 79*(4), 475–480.

Mumford, M. D. (1983). Social comparison theory and the evaluation of peer evaluations: A review and some applied implications. *Personnel Psychology, 36*(4), 867–881.

Murphy, K. R., & Cleveland, J. N. (1991). *Performance appraisal: An organizational perspective.* Boston, MA: Allyn & Bacon.

Murphy, K. R., & Cleveland, J. N. (1995). *Understanding performance appraisal: Social, organizational, and goal-oriented perspectives.* Newbury Park, CA: Sage.

National Policing Improvement Agency (NPIA). (2011). *Rapid evidence assessment of performance and development review systems summary report.* London, UK: NPIA.

Oettmeier, T. N., & Wycoff, M. A. (1997). *Personnel performance evaluations in the community policing context.* Washington, DC: Police Executive Research Forum.

Palmer, J. K., & Loveland J. M. (2008). The influence of group discussion on performance judgments: Rating accuracy, contrast effects, and halo. *Journal of Psychology, 42*(2), 117–130.

Patten, T. H., Jr. (1977). *Pay: Employee compensation and incentive plans.* London, UK: Free Press.

Prien, E. P., & Hughes, G. L. (1987). The effect of quality control revisions on mixed standard scale rating errors. *Personnel Psychology. 40*(4), 815–823.

Pulakos, E. D. (1997). Rating of job performance. In D. L. Whetzel & G. R. Wheaton (Eds.), *Applied measurement methods in industrial psychology* (pp. 291–317). Palo Alto, CA: Davies-Black Publishing.

Roberts, G. E. (1998). Perspectives in enduring and emerging issues in performance appraisal. *Public Personnel Management, 27*(3), 301–320.

Slaughter, J. E., & Greguras, G. J. (2008). Bias in performance ratings: Clarifying the role of positive versus negative escalation. *Human Performance, 21*(4), 414–426.

Swank, C. J., & Conser, J. A. (1983). *The police personnel system.* New York, NY: John Willey & Sons.

Tziner, A., Kopelman, R., & Joanis, C. (1997). Investigation of raters' and ratees' reactions to three methods of performance appraisal: BOS, BARS, and GRS. *Revue Canadienne des Sciences de l' Administration, 14,* 396–404.

Van Maanen, J. (1976). Breaking in: Socialization to work. In R. Dubin (Ed.), *Handbook of work, organization, and society* (pp. 67–130). Chicago, IL: Rand McNally.

Van Meter, D. J. (2001). Evaluating Dysfunctional Police Performance. Springfield, IL: Charles C Thomas.

Walsh, W. F., & Donovan, E. J. (1990). *The supervision of police personnel: A performance based approach.* Dubuque, IA: Kendall/Hunt Publishing Company.

Wanguri, D. (1995). A review, an integration, and a critique of cross-disciplinary research on performance appraisals, evaluations, and feedback: 1980–1990. *Journal of Business Communications, 32*(3), 267–272.

Wexley, K. N., & Yukl, G. A. (1984). *Organizational behavior and personnel psychology.* Homewood, IL: Richard D. Irwin.

Whetstone, T. S. (1994). Subordinates evaluate supervisory and administrative performance. *The Police Chief, 61*(6), 57.

Whisenand, P. M., & Rush, G. E. (1998). *Supervising police personnel: The fifteen responsibilities.* Upper Saddle River, NJ: Prentice Hall.

Wilson, O. W. (1963). *Police administration.* New York, NY: McGraw-Hill.

Wimer, S. (2002). The dark side of 360 degree feedback. *Training and Development,* 37–42.

# 3

# DESIGNING AND USING AN EFFECTIVE POLICE PERFORMANCE APPRAISAL SYSTEM

## Introduction

This chapter will provide features of an effective performance appraisal system. It is crucial to the effective functioning of any organization that it has a system in place that accurately measures employee performance, and one that effectively communicates performance feedback while also motivating improvement and positive changes in performance (Ilgen, 1993). Performance appraisal research has worked to achieve these basic goals.

All human resource systems, including performance appraisals, need to be evaluated for effectiveness (Murphy & Cleveland, 1991). Problems with currently available methods for evaluating performance appraisal systems represent some of the most pressing problems facing practitioners. Clearly, if an organization lacks the ability to assess its personal performance appraisal system, it will be unable to accurately gauge overall organizational performance (Bernardin, Kane, Ross, Spina, & Johnson, 1995).

Performance appraisals are among the most important human resource systems in organizations that represent critical decisions related to human resource actions and outcomes. Unfortunately, most managers and organizations fail to understand the true costs of an ineffective performance appraisal system, and therefore put insufficient effort into fixing the problems associated with it, no matter how obvious. Ineffective appraisal systems can lead to a number of serious problems that negatively impact employee performance and effectiveness of the organization (Judge & Ferris, 1995). Therefore, it is critical for managers to understand the features of an effective performance appraisal system.

### Elements of an Effective Performance Appraisal System

What are the essential features of a "good" performance appraisal system? Research suggests that a good system would be one that is *valid, reliable,* and *practical.* Validity refers to the degree to which an instrument is measuring what it purports to measure. If it is not, the appraisal system promotes wrong work behaviors and creates negative organizational products. In essence, it will cause more organizational harm than good. A valid performance appraisal is well grounded and sound if its criteria are job related and the raters are trained (Bennett & Hess, 2007, p. 489).

Reliability involves the extent to which a measurement gives consistent numerical descriptions of individuals from one time to another or one appraisal to another. Practicality refers both the instrument's acceptability to management and employees, and its user-friendliness, ease of administration and interpretation, and time required for completion (Baker & Holmgren, 1982; Millar, 1990). Police organizations should consider all three characteristics when designing or revising a personal performance appraisal program.

A great deal of research has been conducted in the area of performance evaluation over the years, and experts have provided many useful recommendations that can be used by police managers. For example, they recommend the measurement of employee behaviors instead of characteristics, conducting evaluations more than once per year, and properly training raters (Edwards, 1990; Kozlowski, Chao, & Morrison, 1998). Research suggests that performance appraisals are most likely to be perceived by employees as accurate and fair when: (1) appraisals are conducted frequently, (2) there is a formal system of appraisal, (3) supervisors have a high degree of job knowledge, (4) ratees have an opportunity to appeal ratings, (5) performance dimensions are seen to be highly relevant, (6) action plans are formed for dealing with present weaknesses, and (7) the organizational climate is cooperative rather than competitive (Murphy & Cleveland, 1995).

In a study of the U.S. Navy, Bjerke, Cleveland, Morrison, and Wilson (1987) identified five general characteristics of an effective performance appraisal process: First, they suggested that appraisal processes should gather performance information for clearly defined uses. They recommended not using the same data for different purposes unless the purposes are compatible. For example, using the same data for counseling and as a basis for promotion would be inappropriate. Employees will often criticize or reject information received in counseling if the process uses the same information to support a promotion.

Second, the process should be accepted not only by the organization, but also by the employees and the raters. Third, raters should be trained to help reduce evaluation errors, such as the halo effect and central tendency. The fourth characteristic is that there must be constructive, mutual feedback between supervisors and subordinates integrated into the process if performance improvement or development planning is the ultimate goal.

The process should also be efficient. Efficiency is affected by three factors. First, the format should be simple and concise. Timing, the second factor, should meet organizational goals and provide timely and useful feedback to the employee. The third factor is the importance of the source of information for appraisals.

Coutts and Schneider (2004) offer five of their own components for an effective performance appraisal system. The first is a focus on performance variables rather than on personal characteristics. The second is an opportunity for the employee to have input into the evaluation process, which increases the perceived fairness of the evaluation procedure. Third is to provide feedback to promote employee development. The fourth component is to foster the accomplishment of individual and organizational goals for both the supervisor and employee. The last component is the rater's attainment of task-relevant skills and knowledge, which requires training. Performance appraisal rater training is certainly a vital tool for an objective evaluation. Comprehensive training improves the rater's evaluation skills, such as observational skills, reducing bias, providing constructive feedback, and so forth.

Other researchers have noted the need for a *focus on performance variables rather than on personal characteristics* (Smither, 1998). Evaluations should generally be made in relation to the nature of the job and its responsibilities instead of the personal features of ratees and personality characteristics (Lee, 1985; Rudman, 1995). Personal characteristics have been identified to be subject to various interpretations by managers (Philip, 1990), as they are vague and raters typically cannot come to an agreement on the ratings (Latham & Wexley, 1994). In addition, they are not linked to what an employee has achieved (Grote, 1996). Furthermore, Harris (1988) and Latham and Wexley (1994) have drawn attention to the fact that courts have consistently rejected personal characteristics assessment as the basis of promotion, dismissal, or tenure decisions, as these measures are highly subjective. It is not possible to demonstrate validity and reliability of the ratings; thus, characteristic ratings are not legally defensible (Grote, 1996).

Another important requirement for an effective performance appraisal system is to provide an *opportunity for employees to have input into the evaluation process*, which increases the perceived fairness of the evaluation system (Gilliland & Langdon, 1998). Evans and McShane (1988) report that, with few exceptions, employees have more positive attitudes toward the appraisal when they are given the opportunity to participate. Research has shown that subordinate participation in performance appraisals results in greater satisfaction and work productivity (Wexley, Singh, & Yukl, 1973). Employees will hold more positive attitudes toward their appraisal system when they have an opportunity to state their own opinions (Dipboye & de Pontbriand, 1981). Research clearly demonstrates that user input is a critical factor in the success of a performance appraisal system (Silverman & Wexley, 1984; Bernardin & Beatty, 1984; Roberts, 1992).

Another important feature is to *provide feedback to promote employee development*. It is generally agreed that an effective appraisal system would provide feedback, improve communication (Landy, Zedeck, & Cleveland, 1983; Latham & Wexley, 1994), identify flaws and correct them, and improve ratees' capacity (Cardy & Dobbins, 1994; Murphy & Cleveland, 1995). The more specific the feedback, the more performance improved (Ilgen, Fisher, & Taylor, 1979). Research has shown that police officers want feedback from supervisors and consider feedback as a form of demonstrating confidence in their abilities (Beck & Wilson, 1997). Feedback is desirable for the removal of ambiguity, reinforcing positive experiences, and preventing supervisors from appearing uncaring.

Additionally, a performance evaluation system should be designed to *foster the accomplishment of individual and organizational goals* for both the supervisor and employee. Effective performance appraisal serves to clarify performance standards and expectations (Lowenberg & Conrad, 1998) and provides the medium for supervisors and employees to negotiate mutually agreed-upon goals (Katzell, 1994; Latham & Wexley, 1994). Employees hold a more positive attitude toward their appraisal system when they have the opportunity to discuss objectives and plans (Dipboye & de Pontbriand, 1981).

Another feature of an effective appraisal system is the *rater's attainment of task-relevant skills and knowledge*, which requires training. A comprehensive rater training program is a vital element for an effective performance appraisal system. Unfortunately, most organizations do not dedicate sufficient time and energy to such training (Feldman, 1986; Mohrman, Resnick-West, & Lawler, 1989; Woehr & Huffcutt, 1994). Training should include the role of the organization, rater, ratee, and how the results of performance appraisals are used (Martin & Bartol, 1986). Roberts (1998) argues that a lack of training indicates a lack of commitment in the organization. He notes that evaluators require training in feedback, counseling, interviews, goal setting, and performance standards.

As the foregoing discussion suggests, researchers have identified a very wide range of factors that have been found to influence the effectiveness of an appraisal system. It is very important to note, however, that there is no perfect system or absolute best practice. But, it is possible to sift through this literature and these findings and to use them to suggest certain essential features or best practices in performance appraisal. We must keep in mind, as researchers have argued, that every organization should design its own appraisal instrument and process that supports the organizational goals that it desires to achieve (Greenberg, 1986; Longenecker & Nykodym, 1996). In other words, there is no one-size-fits-all system available to police organizations. Performance appraisal systems and instruments should be carefully designed to suit each organization's particular needs (Latham & Wexley, 1994).

With that caveat, we do offer the following items that we believe should necessarily be contained in all police performance appraisal systems:

- A clear communication of performance expectations. Adequate, poor and superior performance levels must be clearly defined and communicated in advance of the actual appraisal process. Expectations should be clearly set and widely understood by rank and file officers and all supervisory personnel. Criteria measures should be both reliable and valid (Penney, et al., 2011). The criteria for performance and the specific duties and responsibilities associated with each rank must then be explicitly communicated to all members of the organization (Guerra, 2011). This will help to foster objectivity and minimize subjective judgment.
- The focus should be on performance variables rather than on personal characteristics or traits (Smither, 1998; Rudman, 1995; Lee, 1985). In other words, the evaluation must not merely focus upon who or what the employees are. The performance appraisal must specifically identify what the employees *do, achieve* or *accomplish* in relation to stated goals (Manoharan, et al., 2011, p. 724).
- Employees should be given the opportunity to have input into the evaluation process (Gilliland & Langdon, 1998; Evans & McShane, 1988; Silverman & Wexley, 1984; Bernadin & Beatty, 1984; Dipboye & dePontbriand, 1981). Officers of every rank should have an opportunity to review and comment upon the organization's appraisal system. This is most easily done by means of a standing committee to periodically (perhaps bi-annually) review and revise the system. Comments can then be forwarded to senior officials who would take them under advisement. Officers can be selected by their peers to serve upon this committee. In those agencies with collective bargaining agreements, union representative may perform this function. Some agencies might also wish to consider input from other stakeholders, such as representatives from the community.
- Feedback should be provided to employee to promote on-going employee development (Murphy & Cleveland, 1995; Latham & Wexley, 1994; Cardy & Dobbins, 1994; Landy et al., 1983). "Instead of a one-sided rehashing of past performance, [annual] reviews should focus on the future" (Walsh,

2011, p. 15). All employees should have an individualized development plan. This would identify personal goals, such as future training, acquisition of new skills, new assignments, etc. The police organization must ensure that unambiguous career paths are clearly identified for all personnel and that they are linked to specific performance expectations. Recent research suggests that so-called GEN Y employees (i.e., individuals born mid-1970's to early 2000's), in particular, expect and require regular and on-going feedback (Pyrillis, 2011; Townsend, 2011; Inskeep, 2009). It is therefore more important than ever to move beyond providing feedback only during yearly performance evaluations.

- "Participative goal setting" should take place. This is a process whereby supervisors directly ask their employee to describe their performance for the upcoming year. Studies have found that, "when employees themselves have been involved with goal setting and choosing the course of action to be followed by them, they are more likely to fulfill their responsibilities" (Manoharan, et al., 2011, p. 725).

- Appraisals should foster the accomplishment of individual and organizational goals for both the supervisor and employee (Lowenberg & Conrad, 1998; Dipboye & dePontbriand, 1981; Katzell, 1994; Latham & Wexley, 1994; Roberts, 1992). Individual performance appraisals must be directly linked to both unit and organizational goals. The purpose of this is to foster a system of personal accountability and continuous improvement.

- Individual performance appraisal should be linked in some way to rewards (Schachter, 2004). This is somewhat difficult in a civil service system. Nevertheless, appraisal systems can be linked directly to enhanced training opportunities, choice assignments, promotion opportunities, etc.

- Raters should be trained to properly prepare the performance appraisal (Kozlowski, et al., 1998; Woehr & Huffcutt, 1994; Mohrmann, et al., 1989; Feldman, 1986). They must also have a comprehensive and firm grasp of the department's rules, regulations, policies and procedures, as they are incorporated by reference in every performance evaluation. Re-training must occur periodically, so that supervisors maintain their evaluation skills.

- Raters should utilize a formal checklist for preparation of the appraisal and for conducting the post-evaluation interview. This will ensure uniformity of process. The completed checklist, identifying all information sources used and consulted, must become a permanent part of the official file.

- Raters must consult with appropriate parties within the organization to obtain accurate data regarding an officer's: 1) arrest and summons activity; 2) attendance and sick records; 3) training records; 4) use of force history; 5) vehicle accidents; 6) civilian and internal complaints; 7) prior performance evaluations; etc. Such information should be obtained by supervisors and analyzed regularly, not just immediately prior to the formal review process. Ideally, many of these records would be maintained centrally in an Office of Professional Responsibility which would serve, in part, as a quality-control and "early warning" system for detecting actual misconduct or non-feasance of duty. The rater's checklist would be used to ensure that all of these information sources are consulted and used for all performance appraisals.

- The evaluation forms must include an open narrative section for additional comments by the supervisor. While evaluation forms are constructed in such a way as to ensure uniformity, new or unforeseen supervisory issues will always arise. Supervisors must be afforded an opportunity to document and share pertinent performance information that does not fit clearly into any one category. For example, a patrol supervisor might find that subordinates are making appropriate use of the department's radio communications system while on patrol, but that they are also using personal cell phones while on duty. Many agencies are now contending with a new phenomenon; patrol officers who "*self dispatch*" one another via these private cell phone communications. An evaluating supervisor must have an opportunity to explain and document this new problem. An open-ended narrative section of the evaluation report would be the most effective means of noting and correcting this problem.

- The evaluation should obviously consider not only an employee's rank, but their actual assignment. For example, an officer who is serving as an instructor at a recruit academy will obviously have low productivity, in terms of arrests and summonses issued. Similarly, an officer who has recently returned from military or maternity leave, or an officer assigned to a community policing assignment, will likely have fewer arrests and summonses than their peers. The burden is therefore upon the supervisor to take a ratee's assignment and recent history into consideration and to ensure that the evaluation is both fair and performance-based.
- Employees should have an opportunity to appeal rater's appraisal (Murphy & Cleveland, 1995). The appeal process should be stated in writing and should be transparent, so that all parties understand exactly who will review the appraisal, when and how it will be reviewed.

A well-designed and well-executed performance appraisal system of any given organization that includes these elements can have greater efficiency, effectiveness, and improved employee morale.

Many of the foregoing recommendations are *procedural* in nature. That is, they are primarily recommendations about how to design and conduct employee performance evaluations. They neglect to address the *substance* of the evaluations. One is therefore likely to ask, "I understand how to design and conduct the evaluation, but what exactly should I measure? What exactly are the core competencies associated with police work?"

As stated previously, every police agency is unique. Therefore, a cookie cutter approach that attempts to impose a generic performance evaluation model on a department with a unique history and culture is likely to fail. For this reason, police administrators are encouraged to consult the literature, to look to other models, but to liberally make alterations where necessary. We would recommend that the department obtain several examples of evaluation forms from other agencies and choose those portions that appear most relevant and useful. It is unlikely that another department's evaluation form needs to be adopted in its entirety. Rather, the wise police leader will design a comprehensive form that is custom-made for his or her agency.

Police departments should be reluctant to use appraisal forms developed by municipalities (or larger governmental bodies) for general use throughout government service. Many times, police appraisal forms are merely standard forms prepared for appraising the performance of public employees within a variety of government agencies, not just police departments. If this is the case, it is unlikely that the appraisal forms have been properly modified or formatted to address the particular culture of a police organization, or the unique skills and competencies required of an officer or police supervisor. It should be remembered that policing is a very dynamic business and that the requisite skills and duties of police officers continually evolve as new approaches and philosophies, such as the community policing movement, appear and become integral to police work. Police managers must have the ability to create their own appraisal systems, or at least to have substantial input into its development. As a general rule, management always has the authority to set reasonable, clear and achievable performance standards for employees. This authority should not be divested to others, even for the purpose of ensuring uniformity of practice among public agencies. Unnecessary or inappropriate performance measures or forms can lead to a variety of organizational dysfunctions including, but not limited to, poor morale and weak performance.

For those police professionals who feel somewhat frustrated by our reluctance to provide the contents of a one-size-fits-all evaluation form, we offer the following. While it is inherently difficult to identify the personal qualities associated with superior police work (Sanders, 2003), a comprehensive review of representative performance evaluation forms from many different police agencies suggests the following core competencies or work skills associated with the role of police officer:

### Core Competencies of a Police Officer

*Attendance*: Simply stated, police officers must avoid tardiness and unexcused absences.

*Punctuality*: Many collective bargaining agreements address actual "report times" for specific tours. Regardless, it is wise for officers to arrive ready for work several minutes before they are actually expected. This performance dimension may also address timely response to calls for service.

*Communication skills*: Police officers are expected to write and speak clearly and effectively. They are also expected to communicate with colleagues, supervisors, and members of the community in a courteous, tactful, and respectful manner. Information contained in official reports and computer entries should be properly formatted, concise, clear, and accurate. Paperwork should be legible, contain all necessary information, and rarely be returned for correction.

*Cooperation*: This is not merely a personal disposition, characteristic, or attitude. It refers to the officer's ability to work cooperatively and constructively with other officers, supervisors, and the community. Any failure to work collaboratively with others should be documented and the officer should be counseled and retrained in the skills associated with teamwork and team building. Any degree of insubordination cannot be tolerated. It must immediately be addressed.

*Initiative*: Evaluating supervisors should be vigilant to observe and commend instances of personal initiative and self-direction. Conversely, officers should not need to be continually directed or reminded by supervisors to perform ordinary or routine tasks associated with their work role. Ideally, the officer should periodically suggest new methods and approaches to increase personal or organizational efficiency.

*Job knowledge*: Officers should possess a thorough understanding of department rules, regulations, and policies. They should carry out their duties with minimal direction, demonstrate proper use and maintenance of equipment, and prepare forms and make all computer entries in an accurate and complete manner.

*Decision making/judgment*: Ideally, an officer should make work decisions in a prompt, deliberative, and ethical manner. Whether acting individually, or as part of a group, the officer should be fair and decisive. Officers should exhibit composure and clear decision-making skills while under stress.

*Problem-solving skills*: This category typically deals with the officer's ability to make effective short-term and long-term decisions, and to assist colleagues, supervisors, and the community in their decision making. There is often a fine line between deliberation and decisiveness. Officers must make proper use of available time to make correct decisions.

*Professional appearance*: This primarily entails proper use and display of equipment and uniform.

*Safety*: This category includes a variety of safety tactics designed to protect the safety of the officer and others (such as the proper means of conducting a felony car stop, or response to a call of an emotionally disturbed person). It would also include the proper and safe operation of department vehicles, and proper use, care, and maintenance of equipment.

*Time management*: This performance dimension refers to an officer's ability to determine and "budget" available time in an effective manner. Supervisors are trained to review and evaluate the "time on task" for subordinates performing relatively routine tasks. If an officer requires considerably more time to accomplice normal tasks, he or she should receive additional monitoring and training.

*Honesty*: It goes without saying that all police officers must perform their duties with integrity and must avoid even the appearance of impropriety. Many police organizations promulgate or adhere to a formal code of ethics or conduct. In any event, all police officers must be fully aware of their legal and ethical responsibilities and must, at all times, fulfill the duties imposed upon them by law. Police supervisors must remain vigilant and must quickly and decisively respond to any evidence or suggestion of dishonesty or criminality.

Police departments that require additional assistance in connection with their efforts to develop or revise their personal performance appraisal systems should carefully examine the sophisticated appraisal system developed by the Royal Canadian Mounted Police (see, e.g., Catano, Darr, & Campbell, 2007). Departments should also look to the guidelines promulgated by professional accreditation organizations, such as the Commission on Accreditation of Law Enforcement Agencies (CALEA) at www.calea.org.

In an effort to ensure objectivity, all evaluations should also be data based. That is, there should be objective performance data available within official department records to support all managerial judgments and conclusions in the appraisal. Relevant data would include, but would not be limited to, the following: arrest totals; summons and citation activity; attendance records; the number of reports taken and prepared (such as vehicle accident reports, criminal complaint reports, youth referrals, etc.); the number and type of uses of force or investigatory stops conducted; and internal and external complaints. While virtually all modern police agencies compile and undoubtedly have data of this type at their disposal, not every police department mandates that officers self-report their activities via hard copy monthly activity reports. We believe that there is great value in this type of self-reporting system as it serves a check and balance function and ensures personal accountability on the part of all police officers.

Police administrators must be careful, however, not to place too much importance on any one performance metric. The total number of arrests made, for example, is certainly a relevant and important measure, but it is not dispositive. The total number of arrests clearly depends upon an officer's particular assignment and personal situation. For example, an officer assigned to a youth outreach initiative will likely have low arrest numbers, as would the officer who was absent from work for an extended period of time, such as an officer who has missed work due to a line of duty injury or maternity leave. These factors must obviously be taken into consideration when assessing the overall quality of an officer's work. Many would even go so far as to suggest that the superior officer is one who does not have to make an arrest in certain situations. A seasoned officer might be able to diffuse a volatile situation and verbally address a situation that would otherwise escalate to the arrest stage if handled by a less experienced officer. The total number of arrests, or any other measure for that matter, is simply one factor that needs to be taken into consideration with a host of others, before an accurate appraisal of an officer's work can be made.

### Evaluation of Supervisors and Officers Assigned to "Special" Units

Obviously, the above list is not comprehensive. It should, however, serve as a good start for police managers seeking to revise or develop a new performance appraisal system for patrol officers. Obviously, if an officer is assigned to a special unit or assignment, such as a youth officer or domestic violence officer, those assignments would require unique training and skill sets. It goes without saying that an excellent patrol officer might perform miserably as a detective or crime prevention officer.

Police departments should design detailed job descriptions for each of these assignments and be sure to identify the skills that are required over and above the general role of police officer. This cannot be overemphasized; job descriptions must clearly describe all requisite skills and competencies associated with those positions, so that valid performance assessments can be made. Police departments need not re-invent the wheel in this regard. The facilities that provide outside training for officers newly assigned to these positions (such as local police academies) will typically have detailed job descriptions contained in their training materials. It is wise for police organizations to consult and incorporate these materials by reference when designing the job descriptions and evaluation standards for their own personnel performing these roles.

When designing specific job descriptions and performance criteria, police departments should also consult with other agencies to determine the core skills and competencies associated with each role in those agencies.

Similarly, performance standards for supervisors are necessarily different from those of ordinary patrol officers. In addition to those skills associated with the rank of police officer, police supervisors must possess additional skills, such as the ability to:

- Effectively delegate authority;
- To prioritize workload;
- To plan and set goals;
- To budget and conserve resources;
- To properly coordinate and supervise the activities of subordinates; etc.

One would hope that all supervisors would possess superior communication skills, as well as greater knowledge of departmental procedures and guidelines. This is not always the case however. Superiors should be vigilant in reviewing the work of newly-promoted first line supervisors, to monitor both the quantity and quality of work. Any deficiencies regarding oral or written communication skills must be identified and quickly addressed, so as not to cause additional, more significant, operational problems for the entire organization. First line superiors play a critical role in any police organization. One sergeant with extremely poor communication skills can severely restrict an otherwise highly performing unit or department.

Separate performance evaluation forms should be designed for each specific division and rank within the department.

### Field Training

Field training is an extremely critical police function. As such, field training should be separately addressed when considering a comprehensive police performance appraisal system. Probationary personnel must necessarily be subjected to a different type and amount of supervision. The purpose of this scrutiny is frankly to identify problems quickly so that ineffective employees are quickly identified and removed from service.

Field training officers (FTOs) play a very critical role within a police department and should be properly trained and supported (O'Connell & Straub, 2007). Field trainers must have the ability to accurately assess probationary officers under "field conditions," not simply in an academic setting. For this reason, they must be adept at observing, documenting and correcting the behaviors of probationary personnel as the work is actually being performed. Field training evaluations must have a different scope and structure than those of veteran officers.

An excellent guide for designing and guiding field training operations is made available through the Police Training Officer (PTO) program developed and sponsored by the U.S. Department of Justice Community Oriented Policing Services (COPS) office at www.cops. usdoj.gov. This program is a national model for field training that incorporates community policing and problem-solving principles. It serves as an excellent resource for departments attempting to develop specific evaluation methods and criteria for their probationary personnel.

A distinct, more rigorous evaluation system must be in place for the evaluation of probationary personnel (that is, officers who have graduated from the training academy, are now assigned to field commands, but are still on probation). The evaluation of probationary police officers is typically viewed as an extension of the selection and training processes. For that reason, the day-to-day work of probationary officers is scrutinized more thoroughly. Any significant deficiencies can quickly lead to serious discipline, including permanent dismissal from the organization. What might appear as isolated instances of poor performance on the part of a seasoned officer (such as absenteeism, improper use of force, vehicle accident, etc.) can be considered indicative of a more serious pattern of misconduct and an inability to adequately perform on the part of a probationary officer.

Generally speaking, probationary officers should be evaluated on a daily basis. This typically entails written activity reports prepared by FTO's accompanying them in the field. These reports must be clear, candid and factually-based. Evaluation forms should list specific knowledge, tasks and skills that are required of these junior officers. There should also be space provided for narrative descriptions of observations and instructions.

Police departments with superior field training programs typically have several members who are trained and assigned as field training officers. These officers take turns in observing each probationary officer, so as to obtain a number of opinions from different perspectives. Field training officers then regularly meet to jointly discuss the relative progress of each officer. One senior member of the service should be identified to supervise the entire field training program.

While the length of field training varies from department to department, the average period typically lasts from four to six months. Newly hired officers with prior employment in the field of law enforcement (typically referred to as "laterals") require shorter training periods. Ideally, there should be an opportunity to prolong the field training period for certain individuals, if necessary. Accurate and frequent performance appraisal is key to the success of any field training program.

Obviously, field training officers play an essential role in any police organization. In addition to serving a critical performance evaluation function for those under their direct supervision, their very presence and personal conduct conveys the performance expectations of the department. They must lead by example. Unfortunately, "All too frequently, police organizations fail to understand the impact that FTO's have on the professional development of newly assigned officers" (O'Connell & Straub, 2007, p. 65). Since a great deal of personal and professional modeling takes place during this field training period, it is essential to choose FTO's thoughtfully and carefully.

### The Postevaluation Meeting

This is one of the most important but, unfortunately, also one of the most problematic aspects of police performance evaluations. Rarely are police managers properly trained or prepared with respect to the one-on-one performance dialogues that are used to personally relate the contents of an officer's evaluation. Many times, they are not even conducted at all. These meetings are not inherently complicated; they just need to be conducted properly and in conformity with department policy and general legal standards. Managers and their direct reports have to actively participate in order for the process to be effective.

Upon promotion in rank, first-line supervisors in most departments receive some form of basic management skills course. These courses vary in length and content, but rarely there is a significant amount of time expended in connection with postevaluation meetings of subordinates. Frequently, the topic is entirely omitted. It is far more common for newly promoted supervisors to simply be taught how to properly fill out the evaluation forms. They are told that postevaluation meetings are to be conducted, but are typically only provided with brief general instructions that are entirely insufficient.

While these meetings cannot be entirely scripted, they must follow certain basic guidelines. These are not free-form conversations between colleagues. They are a formal means by which the organization communicates its observations and conclusions regarding the employee's work performance. For that reason, supervisors must know what to say during these meetings, as well as what not to say. For example, supervisors should avoid phrases such as "I feel ..." or "I believe...." This can frequently lead to a verbal confrontation between the supervisor and the subordinate. Instead, managers should use phrases like "I observed ..." or "It has been noted that...." This approach is far more direct and useful.

Training for all raters must be conducted well in advance of the actual review period. Supervisors must be advised about inappropriate statements, such as those that lead to confusion, conflict or a violation of applicable law. It is strongly recommended that supervisor training actually include mock post-evaluation interviews. This should be done both at the time of promotion, and during periodic in-service or executive training for supervisors. It is imperative that these communication and leadership skills be properly developed and periodically reinforced.

Supervisors should also consider creating an agenda for the post-evaluation meeting or, at minimum, a check list of items that need to be addressed during the meeting. It is also recommended that supervisors provide a clear summary of all that was said during the meeting. This written record should be maintained as a permanent part of the evaluation. It is essential that supervisors be prepared for these encounters and that they are able to properly recall all that was discussed during these meetings. Such records should be maintained for the entire course of the ratee's career.

As previously stated, it is imperative that all police departments promulgate clear and complete job descriptions for all positions well in advance of any actual evaluation period. Both the written evaluation and the subsequent verbal comments of supervisors must be based upon these stated expectations and actual observations. A supervisor may not introduce a new performance standard or element during the interview. To do so would undermine the entire evaluation process and subject it to unnecessary legal scrutiny. All oral and written comments that are made by the supervisor must be based upon posted expectations.

Feedback and coaching should be provided to police personnel throughout the year, not just during the formal review period. Obviously, if a performance problem is observed outside the normal review period, it must be immediately addressed. When minor problems need to be addressed, a performance dialogue similar to the postevaluation meeting is normally appropriate. At that time, the supervisor can meet with the subordinate to reinforce policy and expectations and to obtain the subordinate's perception of the noted situation/behavior. Both parties can then work to develop a specific performance improvement plan, including the actual date(s) of the allotted performance improvement period. This should be properly documented and conveyed in writing as an official *notice of unacceptable performance.*

A typical performance improvement plan would include specific milestones that must be accomplished by the employee, as well as notification of what the ramifications are for failing to improve to a specified performance level by a specific date. The purpose of these discussions is twofold. Not only are they designed to improve performance that is not meeting expectations, but they are also intended to continuously improve upon performance that *is* currently meeting expectations. Research suggests that "performance increases when goals are specific and challenging, yet attainable" (Heimerdinger & Hinsz, 2008, p. 384). Employees who feel committed to the organization display a "willingness to exert effort on behalf of the organization," a "strong desire to retain membership of the organization," and generally wish to feel as if they have made a personal contribution to the mission and work of the organization (Metcalfe & Dick, 2000, p. 812). They should therefore be carefully coached and directed throughout the year so as to maximize performance.

Obviously, instances of serious misconduct should be addressed via the organization's official internal discipline program and protocols. For this reason, performance measurement systems must work in coordination with their department's internal affairs unit. Ideally, the personal performance appraisal process should include a formal system for recognizing and suitably commending the accomplishments of employees, should be logically linked with the internal affairs function, and should be housed within an office of professional standards.

## Legal Issues Related to Performance Appraisal

There are myriad significant legal issues associated with the preparation and use of police performance evaluations. Indeed, it is likely that an entire volume can be devoted to the exploration and discussion of these issues. Rather than presenting an exhaustive legal treatise on all of these issues, we have identified several that are of immediate significance to the police supervisors preparing these evaluations, as well as the officers receiving them:

1. *The need for accurate job descriptions and clear expectations*: Once again, we cannot overemphasize the importance of having detailed descriptions of the duties and responsibilities associated with each particular rank and role within a police department. A substandard annual or semiannual performance evaluation suggests that an officer's actual performance is at odds with acceptable or minimum standards. Supervisors must therefore be meticulous in recalling and expressing exactly what those standards are. If administrators cannot easily describe what the organization's work expectations are, any supposed evaluations appear arbitrary and capricious.

From a legal standpoint, this could be fatal to the entire evaluation system. Performance targets and expectations must not be a moving target; they must be clearly expressed in advance, then communicated and reinforced throughout the entire organization. This entails not just a clear expression of duties and responsibilities associated with each rank, but a process of individual goal setting. During each review period, employees should collaborate with supervisors to establish individual performance goals for the next review cycle. These annual goals can then be developed into a comprehensive career development plan for the individual. In this way, employees can take ownership for the results of their work, their impact upon the organization, and their own career development.

In general, most employees wish to have a thorough understanding of their employer's expectations, prefer to be actively engaged in their work, and wish to make real contributions to their employer.

Clearly expressed work expectations lead to transparency and personal accountability as all members of the organization will understand clear performance standards that set forth those core competencies associated with each position. Supervisors will find it to be far easier to complete evaluations of their subordinates when clear job descriptions and expectations exist. When they do, supervisors need only to perform "gap analysis," by comparing an employee's actual performance to the desired performance level that is expressed.

If comprehensive and clear job descriptions exist, the next logical step is to identify metrics or measures that will be useful or necessary to the evaluation process.

2. *Personal performance goals or targets must not appear to be quotas*: Despite the near continuous protestations of police commanders, it appears that arrest and ticket quotas do actually exist. While all police departments differ, one must recognize that some agencies do cross the fine line between setting broad personal performance expectations and actually establishing and communicating an exact benchmark target for summonses and arrests. The latter approach has had significant negative repercussions, particularly in the United States.

Consider the case of two Los Angeles police officers who instituted a civil lawsuit against their superiors and employer for retaliating against them for "complaining about alleged traffic ticket quotas" (Blackstein & Rubin, 2011, p. 1). These veteran motorcycle officers sued their department in 2009, "alleging that they had been punished with bogus [i.e., retaliatory] performance reviews, threats of reassignment and other forms of harassment after objecting to demands from commanding officers that they write a certain number of tickets each day" (p. 1). The "number of tickets an officer wrote was recorded on their performance evaluation" (p. 1). Ticket quotas are illegal in California, as they are in other states, as they can cause officers to write unnecessary or fraudulent citations. After trial, "all but one of the twelve jurors in the case sided with the officers, concluding that the officers' reputations and specific employment actions against the officers by the department affected their careers after they reported the misconduct and refused to meet the quotas" (p. 1). The two officers were awarded $2 million in damages.

This case certainly serves as a clear warning to all police departments to construct their performance evaluation programs with care and in such a way that no reasonable person would consider them as imposing explicit quotas. Generally speaking, the violation of traffic laws (or other statutes) must occur naturally. Police departments cannot mandate the number of tickets that are issued by their officers. The actual number of summonses issued will rise and fall naturally; any predetermined level would be viewed as artificial, even if it was supposedly based upon some average that had been observed over time. A far wiser approach is to view a particular officer's summons activity in context by comparing it with that of other officers in the unit or command. Aberrant performance levels (that is, particularly high or low levels) will still be readily apparent, and corrective actions may then be taken as necessary.

What must be avoided at all costs is the imposition of *required* minimum performance numbers. For example, the Fraternal Order of Police challenged a Washington, D.C., Police Department performance evaluation plan that described:

an "unsatisfactory" patrol officer [as] one who, over a four week period, fails to achieve any of the following: one criminal arrest; two traffic or non-criminal arrests; 50 parking tickets, and 10 moving or pedestrian violations. By contrast, the plan define[d] an "outstanding" officer as one who, every four weeks, produces two or more of the following: two or more criminal arrests; six or more traffic or non-criminal arrests; 150 or more parking tickets, and 50 or more moving and pedestrian violations (Anderson & Bouchard, 1985, p. D1).

Not only will police officers react negatively to such a system, but also community members will undoubtedly view such a system as arbitrary and inherently unfair. This problem unfortunately continues to arise in New York and other major cities, as well as smaller police departments in a variety of communities. (Graham, 2012; Parascandola, 2011) It is a significant source of liability and, indeed embarrassment, for many municipalities, for police managers, and for the entire profession.

3. *Raters must at all times remain objective*: It goes without saying that police performance appraisals must be fair and impartial. They must be evidence-based and objective. This proves difficult at times, particularly when the rater does not particularly like the rate. As Wilbanks (2011) notes, it is imperative to

"keep it [the evaluation] impersonal and focused on the job, not on the personality-unless it plays a role in the position" (p. 59). Raters' subjective opinions should be offered judiciously and should be clearly identified as subjective opinion. In addition to having input into the evaluation process, ratees should also be afforded the opportunity to appeal an evaluation by a particular supervisor. Typically, a department will promulgate specific procedures for such appeals, which are usually then performed by the rater's immediate supervisor. Even if an evaluation is not appealed, it should be routinely reviewed at the next highest level to ensure completeness, objectivity, and impartiality. Unfortunately, this is rarely done in police agencies. A periodic inspection or audit of performance evaluations should become part of an agency's overall quality control operations. It can be quite difficult for a supervisor of a relatively small unit to maintain objectivity when preparing the performance evaluations of his or her employees. Nevertheless, there is no option. Supervisors must remain objective at all times regardless of the actual degree of familiarity. Small units can therefore be problematic, particularly when personality conflicts have previously occurred, or where a supervisor has previously reprimanded or disciplined members of the unit. Similarly, even in large agencies or units, a long personal history of association between rater and ratee can severely undermine objectivity.

An interesting case arose in a police department in Florida where a detective challenged the job evaluation he received from a superior officer (a lieutenant) that he had previously arrested. The detective was rated "below standard" in several performance categories. Prior to the arrest, the detective's evaluations were described as being "consistently good" (Weinstein, 1988, p. 3B). Whether the lieutenant actually discriminated or retaliated against the detective is actually beside the point. The critical point here is whether this situation entails an inherent personal conflict. Even if no actual conflict or retaliatory actions can be proven, it is wise for any agency to prevent such situations from occurring in the first place. A far more appropriate response is for the department to have another supervisor perform the detective's evaluation under these circumstances. Police departments should take reasonable steps to avoid even the appearance of impropriety.

4. *Performance records must be maintained and handled in accordance with applicable law*: Police managers would be wise to consider performance evaluation records to be "legal" documents, as they are necessarily part of an employee's permanent personnel/work file. As such, there are explicit laws and rules that govern maintenance and disclosure of these records. Police departments must be meticulous in ensuring that all applicable laws and guidelines are fully complied with.

Even the most competent and scrupulous departments, though, may find themselves at a loss to determine how to properly respond to particular situations. For example, a case that arose in Connecticut established that a "police officer's performance appraisals consisting primarily of supervisors' numerical evaluations are not protected from disclosure by the Freedom of Information Act's (FOIA) exemption as an invasion of the officers' privacy" (Weinstock, 1998, p. 1). As a result of this decision, it was determined that municipal employers must release the performance evaluations of fellow officers to the police union for "use in grievance arbitrations if the matter in arbitration relates to what's in the appraisals" (p. 1). The police department attempted to prevent disclosure of the evaluations of these fellow officers by contending that disclosure of their records would constitute an invasion of their privacy. Both the State Board of Labor Relations and a state superior court rejected the invasion of privacy claim and determined that disclosure was necessary. Employers must therefore be prepared to disclose to third parties the performance evaluations of officers who contest their own evaluation, as well as the evaluations of "peer" or fellow officers who were evaluated at the same time as the appealing officer.

Another difficult situation concerning performance appraisals arose for the Philadelphia, Pennsylvania, Police Department in 1996. An investigative newspaper article disclosed that during a six-year period, the department had fired 82 officers, several of whom "had committed robbery, rape, extortion, drug trafficking and other offenses" (Fazlollah, 1996). Unfortunately, internal department documents disclosed that "almost until the moment it fired them, the department gave those officers top performance ratings—including the murderer" (p. 1). This fact is not only publicly embarrassing, though. Depending upon the particular circumstances of these criminal cases, and whether or not these personnel evaluations were conducted thoroughly and in good faith, the department arguably could have been subjected to civil liability for negligence and improper supervision, if it knew or reasonably should have known about the officers' illegal activities. The point here is that superior performance ratings should not be given out lightly, and police departments should take their duties of supervision and evaluation very seriously.

There are numerous other significant legal issues that can arise naturally in connection with the police performance appraisal process. Suffice it to say that police officials should anticipate them and should act thoughtfully and carefully in all such situations. The wise police manager will consult legal counsel when structuring and operating the personnel evaluation system.

## Conclusion

In this chapter, we discussed the elements of an effective appraisal system. Both practitioners and students of police administration should be keenly aware of these characteristics and essential features, so as to understand what exactly distinguishes the police appraisal process, from performance appraisal generally.

In the following chapter, the items of an effective appraisal system will be compared to items in the systems actually used in the Ankara and Toledo police departments. By selecting two very different organizations, it will be quite interesting to see whether any similarities occur in terms of practices employed and resulting attitudes. By studying two distinct organizations and cultures, perhaps we can identify key issues that will suggest how performance appraisals can be both more effective and more readily received by both raters and ratees.

# References

Anderson, J. W., & Bouchard, J. E. (1985, March 29). D.C. officers criticize ticket, arrest quotas in evaluations. *Washington Post*, p. D1.

Baker, H. K., & Holmgren, S. R. (1982). Stepping up to supervision: Conducting performance reviews. *Supervisory Management*, *27*(4), 20–28.

Beck, K., & Wilson, C. (1997). Police officers' views on cultivating organizational commitment: Implications for police managers. *Policing International Journal of Police Strategies and Management*, *20*(1), 175–195.

Bennett, W. W., & Hess, K. M. (2007). *Management and supervision in law enforcement*. Belmont, CA: Wadsworth/Thomson Learning.

Bernardin, H. J., & R. W. Beatty. (1984). *Performance appraisal: Assessing human behavior at work*. Boston, MA: Kent Publishing Company.

Bernardin, H. J., Kane, J. S., Ross, S., Spina, D. S., & Johnson, D. L. (1995). Performance appraisal design, development, and implementation. In G. R. Ferris, S. D. Rosen, & D. T. Barnum (Eds.), *Handbook of human resource management* (pp. 462–493). Cambridge, MA: Blackwell.

Bjerke, D. G., Cleveland, J. N., Morrison, R. F., & Wilson, W. C. (1987). *Officer fitness report evaluation study* (Navy Personnel Research and Development Center Report, TR 88-4). San Diego, CA: Navy Personnel Research and Development Center.

Blackstein, A., & Rubin, J. (2011, April 12). Officers awarded $2 million: Two from LAPD say they were punished for objecting to an alleged ticket quota. *Los Angeles Times*, p. 1.

Cardy, R. L., & Dobbins, G. H. (1994). *Performance appraisal: Alternative perspectives*. Cincinnati, OH: South-Western.

Catano, V. M., Darr, W., & Campbell, C. A. (2007). Performance appraisal of behavior-based competencies: A reliable and valid procedure. *Personnel Psychology*, *60*(1), 201–230.

Commission on Accreditation of Law Enforcement Agencies (CALEA). www.calea.org

Coutts, L. M., & Schneider, F. W. (2004). Police officer performance appraisal systems: How good are they? *Policing: An International Journal of Police Strategies and Management*, *27*(1), 67–81.

Dipboye, R. L., & de Pontbriand, R. (1981). Correlates of employee reactions to performance appraisals and appraisal systems. *Journal of Applied Psychology*, *66*(2), 248–251.

Edwards, M. R. (1990). An alternative to traditional appraisal systems. *Supervisory Management*, *36*(6).

Evans, E., & McShane, S. L. (1988). Employee perceptions of performance appraisal fairness in two organizations. *Canadian Journal of Behavioral Science*, *20*(2), 177–191.

Fazlollah, M. (1996, April 21). Flawed reviews give top ratings to rogues: The weak job evaluation system in the Philadelphia police department; feeds corruption, experts say, it allows bad officers to go unchecked. *Philadelphia Inquirer*, p. B1.

Feldman, J. M. (1986). Instrumentation and training for performance appraisal: A perceptual-cognitive viewpoint. In K. M. Rowlan & G. R. Ferris (Eds.), *Research in personnel and human resources management* (Vol. 4, pp. 45–99). Greenwich, CT: JAI Press.

Gilliland, S. W., & Langdon, J. C. (1998). Creating performance management systems that promote perceptions of fairness. In J. W. Smither (Ed.), *Performance appraisal: State of the art in practice.* San Francisco, CA: Jossey-Bass.

Greenberg, J. (1986). Determinants of perceived fairness of performance evaluation. *Journal of Applied Psychology, 71*(2), 340–342.

Grote, D. (1996). *The complete guide to performance appraisal.* New York, NY: American Management Association.

Harris, C. (1988). A comparison of employee attitudes towards two appraisal systems. *Public Personnel Management, 17*(4), 443–456.

Heimerdinger, S. R., & Hinsz, V. B. (2008). Failure avoidance motivation in a goal-setting situation. *Human Performance, 21*(4), 383–395.

Ilgen, D. R. (1993). Performance appraisal accuracy: An illusive and sometimes misguided goal. In F. Landy, S. Zedeck, & J. Cleveland (Eds.), *Personnel selection and assessment: Individual and organizational perspectives.* Hillsdale, NJ: Lawrence Erlbaum.

Ilgen, D. R., Fisher, C. D., & Taylor, M. S. (1979). Consequences of individual feedback on behavior in organizations. *Journal of Applied Psychology, 64*(4), 349–371.

Judge, T. A., & Ferris, G. R. (1995). Social context of performance evaluation decisions. *Academy of Management Journal, 36*, 80–105.

Katzell, R. A. (1994). Contemporary meta-trends in industrial and organizational psychology. In H. C. Triandis, M. D. Dunnette, & L. M. Hough (Eds.), *Handbook of industrial and organizational psychology* (Vol. 4, 2nd ed., pp. 1–89). Palo Alto, CA: Consulting Psychologists Press.

Kozlowski, S., Chao, R., & Morrison, R. (1998). Games raters play: Politics, strategies and impression management in performance appraisal. In J. Smither (Ed.), *Performance appraisal: State of the art in practice.* San Francisco, CA: Jossey-Bass Publishers.

Landy, F., Zedeck, S., & Cleveland, J. (1983). *Performance measurement and theory.* Hillsdale, NJ: Lawrence Erlbaum Associates.

Latham, G. P., & Wexley, K. N. (1994). *Increasing productivity through performance appraisal.* Reading, MA: Addison-Wesley.

Lee, C. (1985). Increasing performance appraisal effectiveness. *Academy of Management Review, 10*, 322–332.

Longenecker, C. O., & Nykodym, N. (1996). Public sector performance appraisal effectiveness: A case study. *Public Personnel Management, 25*(2), 151–164.

Lowenberg, G., & Conrad, K. A. (1998). *Current perspectives in industrial/organizational psychology.* Boston, MA: Allyn and Bacon.

Martin, D. C., & Bartol, K. (1986). Training the raters: A key to effective performance appraisal. *Public Personnel Management*, *15*(2), 101–109.

Metcalfe, B., & Dick, G. (2000). Is the force still with you? Measuring police commitment. *Journal of Managerial Psychology*, *15*(8), 812–822.

Millar, K. (1990). Performance appraisal of professional social workers. *Administration in Social Work*, *14*(1), 65–85.

Mohrman, A. M., Resnick-West, S., & Lawler, E. E. (1989). *Designing performance appraisal systems: Aligning appraisals and organizational realities*. San Francisco, CA: Jossey-Bass.

Murphy, K. R., & Cleveland, J. N. (1991). *Performance appraisal: An organizational perspective*. Boston, MA: Allyn & Bacon.

Murphy, K. R., & Cleveland, J. N. (1995). *Understanding performance appraisal: Social, organizational, and goal-oriented perspectives*. Newbury Park, CA: Sage.

O'Connell, P. E., & Straub F. (2007). *Performance-based management for police organizations*. Long Grove, IL: Waveland.

Parascandola, Rocco. (2011). "Cops Slap at Bosses Say Quota Fight Led to Bad Evaluations." *Daily News* (New York), April 11, p. 23.

Philip, T. (1990). *Appraising performance for results*. London, UK: McGraw-Hill.

Police Training Officer (PTO) program. U.S. Department of Justice Community Oriented Policing Services (COPS). Retrieved from http://www.cops.usdoj.gov/default.asp?item = 461

Rayman, Graham. (2012). "PBA: Blame NYPD for Ticket Quotas; Cops Unfairly Targeted by Internal Affairs." *The Village Voice*, May 7, p. 4.

Roberts, G. E. (1992). Linkages between performance appraisal system effectiveness and rater and ratee acceptance: Evidence from a survey of municipal personnel administrators. *Review of Public Personnel Administration*, *12*.

Roberts, G. E. (1998). Perspectives in enduring and emerging issues in performance appraisal. *Public Personnel Management*, *27*(3), 301–320.

Rudman, R. (1995). *Performance planning and review: Making employee appraisals work*. Melbourne, Australia: Pitman Publishing.

Sanders, B. A. (2003). Maybe there's no such thing as a "good cop": Organizational challenges in selecting quality officers. *Policing*, *26*(2), 313–329.

Silverman, S. B., & Wexley, K. (1984). Reaction of employees to performance appraisal interviews as a function of their participation in rating scale development. *Personnel Psychology*, *37*(4), 703–710.

Smither, J. W. (1998). Lessons learned: Research implications for performance appraisal and management practice. In J. W. Smither (Ed.), *Performance appraisal: State of the art in practice* (pp. 537–547). San Francisco, CA: Jossey-Bass.

Weinstein, J. L. (1988, November 12). Detective challenges job evaluation: Sergeant was reviewed by boss he arrested. *St. Petersburg Times*, p. 3B.

Weinstock, K. S. (1998). Personnel appraisals may not be so personal. *Connecticut Employment Law Letter*, *6*(9), 1.

Wexley, K. N., Singh, J. P., & Yukl, G. A. (1973). Subordinate personality as a moderator of the effects of participation in three types of appraisal interviews. *Journal of Applied Psychology, 58*(1), 54–59.

Woehr, D. J., & Huffcutt, A. I. (1994). Rater training for performance appraisal: A quantitative review. *Journal of Occupational and Organizational Psychology, 67.*

# 4

# COMPARATIVE STUDY OF THE PERFORMANCE APPRAISAL SYSTEMS IN ANKARA AND TOLEDO POLICE DEPARTMENTS

## Introduction

We will now examine the Ankara and Toledo Police Departments' appraisal systems very closely. This type of comparative case study will help us explore the degree to which both police departments' performance appraisal systems include those factors that are recognized as important components of the performance appraisal process. Indeed, if they are in fact important components, we should be able to identify them, even within two otherwise distinct police organizations. The analytical strategy used in this research is called pattern matching. This technique is important to help us make comparisons between conceptual propositions and actual empirical patterns (Yin, 2003). Pattern matching is described in the research literature as a useful technique for linking data to propositions (Campbell, 1975). Using this method of pattern matching as a case study methodology, we can compare the performance appraisal systems of these two police departments by matching them to patterns suggested by the best practices.

In this chapter, we will provide a general overview of the Ankara and Toledo Police Departments and their appraisal practices. After presenting a brief overview of the organizational structure of the Turkish National Police and Ankara Police Department, the performance appraisal system used in this organization will be closely examined. A subsequent section in this chapter will provide general information about the organizational structure of American policing and investigate the Toledo Police Department's appraisal system in detail. Finally, this chapter will conclude with a comparison and discussion of the two police departments' appraisal procedures.

### Turkish National Police (TNP) Organization

Turkey is a highly centralized country. This can be felt throughout the country's public services, even within the society and social life itself. The police organization is no exception to this generalized atmosphere of centralization (Cevik, Goksu, Filiz, & Gul, 2010). Turkey has one centralized national police organization, with a structure and authority that are somewhat difficult to understand.

The Turkish National Police (*Emniyet Genel Mudurlugu*) operate under the country's Ministry of Interior. The director general of the TNP is nominated by the minister of interior, appointed by the prime minister, and approved by the president of Turkey. The headquarters of Turkish National Police is located in Ankara, and it coordinates the central departments and provincial police departments in 81 different cities throughout Turkey. The chief of the provincial department is accountable to the directorate general of the TNP, as well as to the governor of the province, and is also under the authority of local criminal prosecutors in matters relating to the investigation and prosecution of criminal cases.

As can be seen from Figure 4.1, the headquarters of the TNP consists of one director general, who has five deputies, the director of inspection commission, the head of the National Police Academy, the chief law advisor, and 27 department chiefs. Each department in the headquarters has a connection with the departments in the provinces. Ultimately, the departments in the provinces are under the authority of the chief of the police department of the province. However, certain functions, such as in-service training, education, deployment, and acquisition of new techniques, are performed by or through the headquarters.

On the other hand, there is a provincial structure (see Figure 4.2) that consists of 81 province security departments. The TNP has an overall manpower of more than 200,000 personnel assigned throughout the country. Police departments in the provinces have a similar structure as the headquarters, and each department that exists in the

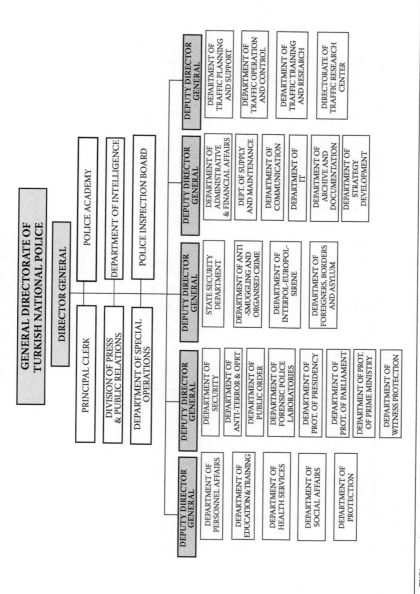

**Figure 4.1**  TNP's organizational structure.

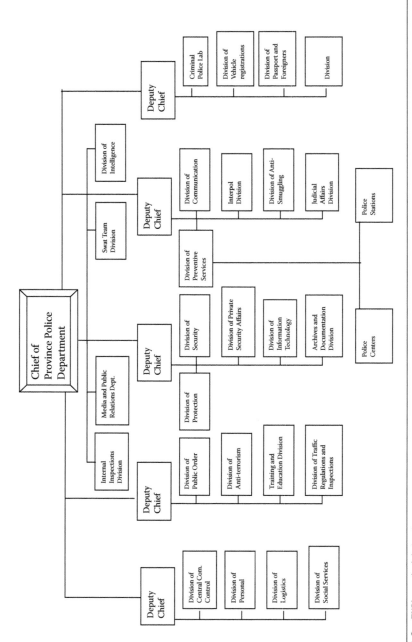

**Figure 4.2**  TNP's provincial structure.

headquarters is also represented in the provinces. A direct line of communication exists between the headquarters and local police departments, and the headquarters has the right and duty to coordinate and direct the provincial units whenever deemed necessary.

The basic training of the nonranking police officers for the organization is accomplished through a police vocational school of higher education (equivalent to police academies in the United States) in 27 provinces throughout Turkey. Cadets admitted to the police vocational school of higher education are selected from among high school graduates. Applicants have to pass an investigative background check, followed by an interview, a written exam, and finally, a physical test or exam. Admitted cadets continue in boarding schools, undergoing training and education for two years (Dogutas, Dolu, & Gul, 2007).

The training of the ranking officers for management levels of the TNP is conducted through the police college (high school), followed by training at the National Police Academy (College of Security Sciences). The police college, a high school level police boarding school, provides four years of high school education without any police training. When students graduate from the police college, almost all of them are admitted to the National Police Academy. The other source of National Police Academy cadets is high school graduates who have not been enrolled at the police colleges. Those who take a national university exam and obtain the required grades are entitled to apply to the police academy, whether or not they have attended the police college. The vast majority of applicants to the National Police Academy, however, are graduates of the police colleges. After successful completion of training at the National Police Academy, cadets start their careers with the rank of sergeant.

The rank structure of the TNP is as follows: police officer, sergeant, lieutenant, captain, major, and chief. Every three or four years the ranking officers receive automatic promotion up to the rank of police major. This of course applies only to those who have performed well, and any misbehavior may lead to delay in promotion. After graduation, a cadet is appointed by the TNP headquarters to one of the 81 city police departments. The first year is the probationary period. After that, the cadet gains all the rights of a police officer.

In Turkey, it is interesting to note that the police operate only within the city and town centers, within the boundaries of municipalities. In rural areas, there is a military force, the gendarmerie, which operates under the minister of interior when performing policing functions, but operates under the general staff for military functions.

### Performance Appraisal System in Ankara Police Department*

In Turkey, the personnel of the police organization are evaluated according to the provisions of Law 657 and the Governmental Officials Performance Evaluation Regulation, a regulation based on this law. The evaluation is the basis for identifying police officers to be promoted, to be retired, to be released from duty, or to have changes of duty or assignment.

Article 10 of the regulations emphasizes the importance of the personnel and performance evaluation files and states that the personnel and performance evaluation files are the main foundation in the determination of a police officer's assignment, his or her rank progression, merit increases, retirement, and dismissals. When police officers change institutions, their personnel and performance evaluation files are sent in complete form to their new institution. The confidential performance evaluation forms of the police officers are completed each year within the second half of the month of December. In order for a performance evaluation report to be prepared, an officer must have worked at least six months together with his or her supervisor.

Supervisors evaluate officers by assigning numerical values of up to 100 points. The average score of the officer is then calculated by dividing the total number of points by the total number of questions. There are four grade categories to be given: bad, average, good, and very good. The points below 60 are considered bad, between 60 and 75 are average, between 76 and 89 are good, and between 90 and 100 are very good performance grades.

In Ankara PD, department chiefs are the first or primary raters and the deputy chiefs are the second raters. If there is a difference between the first and second raters' grade of 10 points or more, then the chief of police has the right to make a final decision.

---

* Starting from May 2012, a newly developed performance appraisal system will be used at the Turkish National Police Organization.

Officers can only appeal their grade if they receive a bad evaluation, which is below 60 points. When an officer receives a bad grade two years in a row, he or she is assigned to another supervisor. If the officer receives a third bad grade, he or she is then dismissed from duty. By contrast, if an officer receives a very good grade for six years consecutively, he or she then becomes eligible for rewards and meritorious consideration.

Interestingly, officers can only learn their evaluation grades when they receive a bad grade (below 60 points). However, the Freedom of Information Act, which was enacted in 2004, allows employees to learn their grades if they make a formal application or request to their departments. If the officers are not pleased with their grades, they can apply to the court.

Raters evaluate police officers in two categories. The first category is an evaluation of the officer's personal characteristics, such as intelligence level, honesty, confidentiality, physical appearance, and bad habits, such as alcohol abuse or gambling. Raters write their comments in the spaces provided in the evaluation form. As anyone can clearly see, these criteria are very subjective and very much open to varied interpretation.

The second category of evaluation is the officer's job knowledge (responsibility, loyalty, professional knowledge, discipline, impartiality, etc.). There are two additional sections in the evaluation form. The first is an evaluation of the supervisory skills (only for ranking officers), and the other is only for employees who are assigned to duty abroad.

Turkish law allows government agencies to include additional criteria in the job knowledge section of the evaluation form, but only upon obtaining approval from the National Personnel Department. Accordingly, the TNP added the following two criteria: maintenance and protection of the equipment and weapons and the ability of using them when necessary, and marksmanship.

### Police Organization in the United States

Unlike the structure in Turkey, where law enforcement is maintained by a national police agency, policing in the United States is highly decentralized. Police in the United States are organized at the federal, state, and local levels (Souryal, 1995; Bennett & Hess, 2007).

Currently, there are approximately 18,500 police departments in the United States. Each of these, for the most part, operates independently and autonomously.

At the federal level, there are national agencies like the Federal Bureau of Investigation (FBI), the Drug Enforcement Administration (DEA), the Secret Service, and so forth. Although their jurisdiction covers the entire country, their authority is limited to certain crimes. At the state level, there are 50 state police departments in the continental United States. All have jurisdiction only within their states. Generally, state police are organized as highway patrols, such as the Ohio Highway Patrol or the New York State Troopers. At the local level, there are municipal police departments and sheriff's offices. These local departments provide most of the police service in the United States.

As a result, the structure of police in the United States is extremely fragmented. The following is a general summary of American police agencies at different levels of jurisdictions:

- 12,501 local police departments
- 3,063 sheriff's offices
- 1,733 special jurisdiction agencies (parks, schools, etc.)
- 50 primary state law enforcement agencies (Bureau of Justice Statistics, 2011)

Generally speaking, police officers in the United States are fairly well educated. By 2003, 81% of all U.S. police departments required at least a high school degree to become a police officer. Nine percent required at least two years of college, and 1% required a four-year college degree (Bureau of Justice Statistics, 2003). These percentages have increased in recent years.

The source of nonranking police officers for any police agency in the United States is the police academies, located throughout the country. Academy training in the United States is provided at the federal, state, and local levels. At the national level, there is an FBI academy, and there are various federal law enforcement training centers. At the state level, each state maintains its own training academy. Training periods vary from 12 to 26 weeks. At the local level, most large metropolitan cities have their own academy. Some universities operate police training academies as well. All local or state level academies must meet minimum requirements established by state police training commissions (Marinen, 1997).

In Ohio, for example, the Ohio Peace Officer Training Commission was established in 1965 by the Ohio General Assembly and placed in the Office of the Attorney General. The commission's primary objective was and continues to be the improvement of the professional capabilities of Ohio peace officers, through very careful oversight of law enforcement training within the state. The commission requires a total of 550 hours of police training. The Ohio State Highway Patrol operates its own academy. Its minimum requirement is a total of 1,071 police training hours (OPOTC, 2002).

The Toledo Police Department is a municipal police department responsible for policing the City of Toledo. Toledo is located in Lucas County in northwestern Ohio. It has a population of 313,619, which makes it the fourth largest city in Ohio and the 57th largest in the United States (City of Toledo, 2007). The Toledo Police Department has a total of 799 personnel, 686 of whom are sworn police personnel. The department is also an accredited law enforcement agency. The Toledo Police Department's organizational structure, as it appeared in 2007, is provided in Figure 4.3.

### Performance Appraisal System in Toledo Police Department

The Toledo Police Department's performance appraisal system is intended to serve as a feedback mechanism for its employees, providing information on individual levels of performance. Evaluations are not used in promotion or as a step in the discipline process. The goal of the appraisal is to help employees improve their performance and assist in their personal development; positive professional development is the key purpose (Supervisor's Guide to Performance Evaluation Systems, 2005). This following information is taken from the Toledo Police Department's *Standard Operating Guidelines* (2005) and *Supervisor's Guide to Performance Evaluation Systems* (2005).

Formal evaluations are completed on patrol officers in this department every June and December of each calendar year. Officers are advised of their evaluating supervisor in early January each year, or immediately upon reassignment. When overall performance is

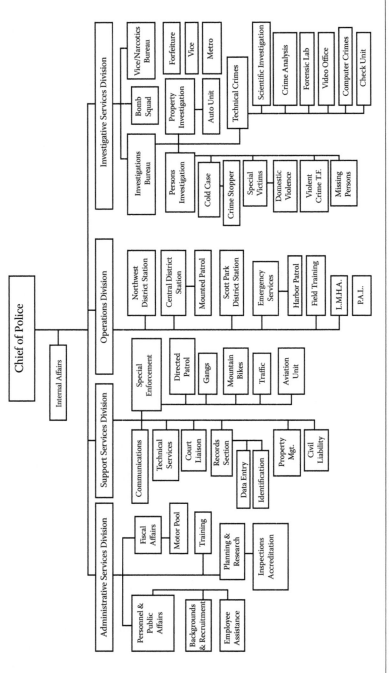

**Figure 4.3**   Organizational structure of Toledo Police Department.

deemed to be unacceptable, the employee is notified in writing at least 90 days prior to the formal evaluation (March and September). The notification may be in memo form and includes the performance dimension, a description of deficient performance, and suggestions for improvement.

At the conclusion of the rating period, supervisors counsel employees in the following areas:

- Results of the performance evaluation that has just been completed
- The level of performance expected and rating criteria or goals for the new reporting period
- Career counseling relative to such topics as advancement, specialization, or training appropriate for the employee's position

Once the interview is completed, the officer and the supervisor sign the evaluation form. A copy of the evaluation is then given to the officer. The original is maintained in the employee's personnel file. Following the review of the form, the supervisor and the employee jointly complete the goal setting/action planning form.

The evaluated employee is granted the right to make a formal appeal concerning the evaluation. An appeal form is attached to the performance evaluation form for easy access. This form allows the officer filing the appeal to make additional comments about the evaluation, such as offering explanations for performance, or complaining about specific aspects of the evaluation process itself.

Due to the wide variety of assignments within the department, a number of different instruments have been created by police administrations to more closely match those varied assignments. Identified performance dimensions are different for the following units: directed patrol, gang units, investigative services, operations division, vice/metro, and patrol. These various evaluation instruments were created with and through the active participation of those who will be evaluated, covering areas of performance they believe important to their function. It is important to emphasize that the Toledo Police Department did not impose one standard evaluation form upon the entire department. It tailored the forms to the units, with the active input of the officers being evaluated.

All evaluations of department personnel are then completed online, utilizing a custom-designed software program (Microsoft FoxPro) that is based upon the mixed standard method of assessment. The evaluation form consists of ratings on general and job-specific dimensions for specific ranks and assignment. The standard dimensions evaluated are officer safety, laws and ordinances, writing skills, verbal communications skills, cooperation/relations with peers, dependability/attendance, beat knowledge/problem solving, appearance, initiative/efficiency, relations with public/demeanor, mediation skills, and department policies and procedures. Supervisors rate the performance of officers in these 12 dimensions on a seven-position graphical scale that is divided into three primary sections:

- Above-average performance: Exceeds expectations.
- Acceptable: Expected level of performance.
- Below standard: Does not meet expectations.

Within each of these three sections is a descriptive statement that identifies real-life job examples of behaviors that an employee might display if he or she were exceeding expectations, meeting expectations, or not meeting job expectations. It is required that each rating that indicates performance not meeting or exceeding expectations be explained through written examples of employee behavior. This is the most important part of the evaluation, as it gives substance to what would otherwise be a subjective rating. It provides descriptive examples of why the employee was rated as he or she was and illustrates what steps are necessary for improvement.

## Comparison and Conclusion

These two police organizations have very different methods to appraise the quantity and quality of work being performed by their employees. The Turkish National Police Organization uses generic evaluation forms—standard forms that are used to evaluate all public employees in the government agencies, not just the police. There is no feedback provided unless an employee receives a negative evaluation (59 points or less). Not surprisingly, this rarely occurs. Department chiefs are the evaluators. They do not receive training about how to conduct the evaluation. Their lack of training in evaluation procedures contributes to the generally negative opinions held by the supervisors. Supervisors have very little ownership of, or support for, their department's performance system. The manner in which these evaluations are conducted clearly calls into question the validity of the entire appraisal process.

On the other hand, the Toledo Police Department has designed its own performance evaluation form. Performance criteria are different for each unit in the department. At the end of the rating period, supervisors meet with and counsel their officers. Formal evaluations are completed twice a year, every June and December. Immediate supervisors evaluate the officers, not individuals situated further up the chain of command. Supervisors also receive training on how to evaluate the officers effectively.

A personal characteristic rating system is the process most criticized by functional level employees in a police organization, since it is typically very subjective and based more on perceptual personality than on actual job performance (Coleman, 1995). The TNP uses the Graphic Rating Scale (GRS). Supervisors use evaluation instruments that employ broadly defined traits as performance criteria. Some of the typical traits and personal characteristics listed on the form are honesty, reliability, bad temper and behavior, and orderliness and attentiveness. Obviously, such terms are very much open to interpretation. They are vague, subjective, and difficult to readily identify. As a result, evaluations can become virtually meaningless and will be of very little practical use. Research also indicates that if the performance measures are not relevant with the employee's job, this more likely increases the employee's dissatisfaction from the performance appraisal process (McGivern & Ferlie, 2007; Narcisse & Harcourt, 2008).

However, the Toledo Police Department's evaluation form consists of ratings on general and job-specific dimensions. Work behavior appraisal is how actual performance actions in the position are assessed and rated. The ratings are based on tangible behaviors that can be gauged and compared to other employees performing the same or very similar tasks. Most police organizations that utilize such a process develop them based on job analysis of incumbents in the position (Coleman, 1995). The Toledo Police Department's appraisal system is based on a commonly used format called the Behavioral Anchored

Rating Scale (BARS). The BARS format is designed to provide ratings that are based on job-relevant behaviors that are important to a healthy and productive work environment. The BARS approach gets away from measuring subjective personal characteristics. Instead, it measures observable, critical behaviors that are related to specific job dimensions (Bopp & Whisenand, 1980). This is a key difference that distinguishes useful performance evaluations from ineffective ones. Evidence from police organizations suggests that anchored rating systems are related to overall satisfaction from the performance appraisal process (Lilley & Hinduja, 2007).

The Toledo Police Department provided an opportunity for employees to have input into the development of the appraisal process. By contrast, TNP used, and continues to use, a generic evaluation instrument designed to evaluate *all public employees* in government service. The Turkish officers therefore had no involvement in the creation of their appraisal form. It is widely understood among TNP officers that the evaluation form used was not designed by police officers, for police officers. This severely limits its effectiveness.

Research clearly demonstrates that user input is a critical factor in the success of any performance appraisal system (Silverman & Wexley, 1984; Bernardin & Beatty, 1984; Roberts, 1992). Perhaps most importantly, such input increases the perceived *fairness* of the evaluation system (Gilliland & Langdon, 1998; Cawley, Keeping, & Levy, 1998; Kavanagh, Benson, & Brown, 2007; Narcisse & Harcourt, 2008; Mamatoglu, 2008). Objectivity and fairness are continually identified as necessary characteristics of any performance appraisal system.

Traditional appraisal approaches typically suffer from two fatal flaws: frequent use of irrelevant criteria and extreme subjectivity. Careful supervisory and organizational oversight has been found to significantly reduce this problem, through the development of reasonable and carefully drawn key job elements, measurable job standards, and reasonable performance appraisal criteria (Swank & Conser, 1983). The only real question is: Will the organization encourage or allow this type of input?

Completely closed performance appraisal systems, in which employees do not see or have any access to their own performance appraisal forms, have become extremely rare. Most appraisal systems have built-in procedures to make sure that employees have an opportunity to review their completed performance appraisal forms (Anderson, 1993). The Turkish National Police has a closed performance evaluation system in which officers do not receive feedback, unless it is a negative evaluation (59 points or below).

One of the major flaws of the appraisal system in the Ankara Police Department is that it relies upon a secret evaluation process, with feedback provided only in case of a negative appraisal. This secret appraisal system does not allow officers to learn about their mistakes and weaknesses. In order to be able to benefit from the performance evaluation, the results of the performance evaluation should be openly shared with the officers and feedback should be provided to them. Through the application of an open evaluation system in the police organization, the employees will be able to know their deficiencies and will have the possibility to correct and improve them.

According to Article 16 of the Governmental Officials Performance Evaluation Regulation, personnel receiving a grade of 59 or less are deemed to have received a negative performance evaluation and the employee is then warned according to a procedure mentioned in Article 21. An interesting question is: What happens when an employee's average performance evaluation is, for example, 60? Such a person has performed considerably worse than his or her peers. Would not the supervisors, as well as the employee, wish to know why? What specifically is the problem? What is the cause? All noted performance deficiencies need to be clearly explained. Specific areas for improvement need to be identified, as well as suggestions for correcting deficiencies.

In the Toledo Police Department, supervisors meet with the officer being evaluated, to discuss the evaluation. During this meeting, all performance dimensions and scores are reviewed and discussed. The supervisor provides specific examples of behaviors displayed by the officer that resulted in particularly unsatisfactory or outstanding evaluations. Such behaviors must be documented. The officer and supervisor then discuss the officer's general strengths and developmental needs for the purpose of improvement. They also agree on a set of developmental goals (see generally Chiodo, 2010).

Employees simply will not benefit from the evaluation process unless the results of the performance evaluation are openly shared with the officers and clear feedback regarding their performance is

**Table 4.1**   A Comparison of Items in Performance Appraisal Systems

| ITEMS | BEST PRACTICES | ANKARA PD | TOLEDO PD |
|---|---|---|---|
| Purpose | Personnel development | Administrative decisions only | Personnel development only |
| Method | NA | Graphic Rating Scale (GRS) | Behavioral Anchored Rating Scale (BARS) |
| Source | Immediate supervisor | Department chief | Immediate supervisor |
| Frequency | More frequently | Once a year | Twice a year |
| Base | Job performance | Personal characteristics | Job performance |
| Feedback | Yes | No | Yes |
| Appeal | Yes | No (only when it is negative) | Yes |
| Rater training | Yes | No | Yes |
| Accomplishment of individual and organizational goals | Yes | No | Yes |
| Provide an opportunity for employees to have input into the evaluation process | Yes | No | Yes |

provided. Employees must know their deficiencies and have the possibility to correct and improve them.

It is interesting to note that the Turkish system requires evaluators to either award a score of 100 points to an employee in the areas of impartiality and respect to human rights, or commence an investigation. Obviously, the vast majority of officers receive a perfect score in these areas. Such a practice provides little useful information and undermines the legitimacy of the entire evaluation process.

Using the method of pattern matching suggested by Yin (2003), Table 4.1 compares the Ankara and Toledo Police Departments' performance appraisal systems with the best practices model presented in Chapter 3.

As discussed earlier and can be seen from Table 4.1, considerable distinctions exist between the two police departments' appraisal systems. While the Toledo Police Department's appraisal system is clearly more similar to the best practices drawn from the literature, the question still remains as to whether employees in the system are more or less satisfied with that performance appraisal system. Chapter 5 seeks to determine under which appraisal system employees are more satisfied.

# References

Anderson, G. C. (1993). *Managing performance appraisal systems.* Cambridge, MA: Blackwell.

Bennett, W. W., & K. M. Hess. (2007). *Management and supervision in law enforcement.* Belmont, CA: Wadsworth/Thomson Learning.

Bernardin, H. J., & R. W. Beatty. (1984). *Performance appraisal: Assessing human behavior at work.* Boston, MA: Kent Publishing Company.

Bopp, W., & Whisenand, P. (1980). *Police personnel administration* (2nd ed.). Boston, MA: Allyn and Bacon.

Bureau of Justice Statistics. (2003). *Local police departments, 2003.* Retrieved from http://www.ojp.usdoj.gov/bjs/pub/pdf/lpd03.pdf

Bureau of Justice Statistics. (2011). *Census of state and local law enforcement agencies, 2008.* U.S. Department of Justice, Office of Justice Programs.

Campbell, D. (1975). Degrees of freedom and the case study. *Comparative Political Studies, 8,* 178–185.

Cawley, B., Keeping, L., & Levy, P. (1998). Participation in the performance appraisal process and employee reactions: A meta analytic review of field investigations. *Journal of Applied Psychology, 83*(4), 615–633.

Cevik, H. H., Goksu, T., Filiz, O., & Gul, S. K. (2010). *Guvenlik yonetimi* [Security management]. Ankara, Turkey: Seckin Publishing.

City of Toledo. (2007). Retrieved April 2007 from http://www.ci.toledo.oh.us

Coleman, J. L. (1995). *Operational mid-level management for police.* Springfield, IL: Charles C Thomas Publisher.

Dogutas, C., Dolu, O., & Gul, S. K. (2007). A comparative study of the police training in the United States, United Kingdom and Turkey. *Turkish Journal of Police Studies, 9*(1–4), 1–20. Retrieved from http://www.pa.edu. tr/objects/assets/content/file/dergi/68/1-20.pdf

Gilliland, S. W., & Langdon, J. C. (1998). Creating performance management systems that promote perceptions of fairness. In J. W. Smither (Ed.), *Performance appraisal: State of the art in practice.* San Francisco, CA: Jossey-Bass.

Governmental Officials Performance Evaluation Regulation (Law 657). Turkey.

Kavanagh, P., Benson, J., & Brown, M. (2007). Understanding performance appraisal fairness. *Asia Pacific Journal of Human Resources, 45*(2), 132–150.

Lilley, D., & Hinduja, S. (2007). Police officer performance appraisal and overall satisfaction. *Journal of Criminal Justice, 35,* 137–150.

Mamatoglu, N. (2008). Effects on organizational context (culture and climate) from implementing a 360-degree feedback system: The case of Arcelik. *European Journal of Work and Organizational Psychology, 17*(4), 426–449.

Marinen, O. (1997). Police training in a democracy. *Issues of Democracy USIA Electronic Journal, 2*(4).

McGivern, G., & Ferlie, E. (2007). Playing tick-box games: Interrelating defenses in professional appraisal. *Human Relations, 60*(9), 1361–1385.

Narcisse, S., & Harcourt, M. (2008). Employee fairness perceptions of performance appraisal: A Saint Lucian case study. *International Journal of Human Resource Management, 19*(6), 1152–1169.

Ohio Peace Officer Training Commission (OPOTC). (2002). *Commander manual for peace officer basic training.* Columbus, OH.

Roberts, G. E. (1992). Linkages between performance appraisal system effectiveness and rater and ratee acceptance: Evidence from a survey of municipal personnel administrators. *Review of Public Personnel Administration, 12.*

Silverman, S. B., & Wexley, K. (1984). Reaction of employees to performance appraisal interviews as a function of their participation in rating scale development. *Personnel Psychology, 37*(4), 703–710.

Souryal, S. (1995). *Police organization and administration* (2nd ed.). Cincinnati, OH: Anderson Publishing.

*Standard operating guidelines.* (2005). Toledo Police Department, OH.

*Supervisor's guide to performance evaluation systems.* (2005). Toledo Police Department, OH.

Swank, C. J., & Conser, J. A. (1983). *The police personnel system.* New York, NY: John Wiley & Sons.

Yin, R. (2003). *Case study research: Design and methods* (3rd ed.). Beverly Hills, CA: Sage Publications.

# 5

## POLICE ATTITUDES TOWARD PERFORMANCE APPRAISAL SYSTEMS

### A Survey of Ankara and Toledo Police Departments

### Introduction

In this chapter, using identical surveys in Ankara and Toledo Police Departments, we will examine the officers' perception of the performance appraisal system and explore whether there is a relationship between the officers' rank, level of education, gender, years of service, age, and their perceptions of the evaluation system. The principal focus is to examine how rank-and-file officers in Ankara and Toledo Police Departments perceive the performance appraisal process in their organizations. This chapter will also present the research design and describe the development of the survey instrument, the hypotheses to be tested, the methods used to analyze the data, and the findings of the research.

### Perception of the Performance Appraisal System

Most research on the performance appraisal process throughout the 1970s and 1980s focused on raters and the rating process. A considerable amount of research was conducted on rating accuracy, psychometric issues, and instrumentation issues (Ilgen, 1993; Latham, 1986). Despite the abundance of rating research and practical recommendations for making accurate ratings, there still appears to be considerable dissatisfaction among employees (both raters and ratees) about the performance appraisal process (Bernardin, Kane, Ross,

Spina, & Johnson, 1995; Hughes, 1990). This is a troublesome fact for all organizations.

In response, the 1990s were characterized by a distinct shift in research emphasis from studies of rater accuracy and psychometric measures to themes of employee reactions toward performance appraisal as indicators of system satisfaction and efficacy (Latham, Skarlicki, Irvine, & Siegel, 1993). Murphy and Cleveland (1995) referred to employee reaction to appraisals as one class of neglected criteria that might be considered in evaluating performance appraisal systems. Bernardin and Beatty (1984) suggested that employee reactions to performance appraisal systems are usually better indicators of the overall viability of a system than the more narrow psychometric indices. A performance appraisal system can be psychometrically sound in design and construction, but still be wholly ineffective in practice due to resistance or lack of acceptance on the part of users. Thus, the effectiveness of a system is particularly contingent on the attitudes of the system users, both raters and ratees (Roberts, 1990). While internal support does not guarantee success for an otherwise weak appraisal system, resistance will ensure failure of virtually any system.

The success of the appraisal systems may well depend on ratees' perceptions of fairness and reactions to essential aspects of the evaluation process (Jawahar, 2007). There is a general consensus among performance appraisal researchers that the assessment of employees' reactions to performance appraisals is important for appraisal system acceptance by the users of the system and for the utility of those appraisals (Keeping & Levy, 2000). Murphy and Cleveland (1995) suggest that researchers should consider the rating context before attempting to analyze or evaluate the effectiveness of ratings or rating systems. Research has included measures of employee attitudes toward performance appraisal and system acceptance and rater and ratee satisfaction in the appraisal process (Roberts, 1990). Consistent with this research trend, we will examine reactions of employees to the performance appraisal process in the Ankara and Toledo Police Departments. Examining reactions to performance appraisals is important because appraisals continue to be used for a wide variety of human resource functions. Since many personnel decisions are influenced by performance appraisal ratings, employee reactions should be given careful consideration.

## Methodology

### Questionnaire

This research has been funded by Research and Graduate Studies of Kent State University (KSU). The researcher received the "Excellence in Research" award from the Graduate Student Senate, Kent State University. This research has also been approved by the Institutional Review Board of Kent State University. In the data collection process, the researcher followed the procedures of this board, which included informed consent, confidentiality, and so forth. At the beginning of the questionnaire an introduction explained the goal, scope, and benefits of the survey. Thus, the participants' attention is drawn to the questionnaire. In addition, it is stated that the information obtained shall be confidential and that there is no obligation to provide identification. Thus, the real opinions and inclinations of the personnel could be better identified.

The questionnaire form (see Appendix A), which was distributed via convenience samples to police personnel who work in Ankara and Toledo Police Departments, consists of three sections. The first section includes questions on demographic information. The respondents were asked to report their gender, age, education, years of service, and current rank. In addition to these, ethnicity, current assignment, and current district were added to the Toledo survey instrument. The second section contains nine items measuring the respondent's perceptions of the performance appraisal system, which are considered to be indicators of employee satisfaction with the overall performance appraisal process.

Part 3 includes 12 statements regarding recommendations for the performance appraisal system. In addition, there are three questions about the bases of the appraisal (job performance, personality characteristics), sources of appraisal (direct supervisor, peers, etc.), and frequency of appraisal (six months, one year, etc.). Finally, there was an open-ended question for the respondents who wished to provide additional comments about their performance appraisal system.

Respondents were asked to indicate the extent to which they agreed with each statement on a 5-point Likert scale: 1 = strongly disagree, 2 = disagree, 3 = neutral, 4 = agree, 5 = strongly agree. Higher values mean higher support for the statements.

Data for this research were collected from police officers and supervisors in Ankara and Toledo Police Departments. The data from Ankara PD (n = 453) and Toledo PD (n = 296) were merged and a department identifier variable (dummy variable) was created. All the analyses are made based on the merged data set (n = 749).

It is argued in the literature that the larger the sample size, the greater the statistical accuracy of the results (Schutt, 2006). The sample size of Ankara PD and Toledo PD is large enough in terms of the statistical criteria. Thus, it provides sufficient statistical evidence to allow careful, reasoned inferences to the general population of the agency. The following sections will explain the data collection procedures in both police departments.

*Data Collection*

*Ankara PD*   In Ankara PD, the questionnaires were distributed to 500 subjects via convenience sample in the summer of 2001. A total of 453 subjects completed the questionnaire for a response rate of 90%. According to the data of the Personnel Affairs Department of the Ankara Police Department, as of the year 2001, the department had a total of 12,459 sworn personnel. The sample for this study constitutes 3.6% of the law enforcement population in the department.

A draft of the questionnaire form was pretested with 40 employees in the Ankara Police Department to fine-tune the instrument for a larger sample. On this basis, a number of questions were revised in order to ensure greater clarity. Furthermore, a number of questions were deleted and some were added and the questionnaire was prepared for distribution. For example, the term *performance appraisal* was used in the original instrument. However, some of the respondents were not sure whether that term referred to *registry report*, which is commonly used instead of *performance appraisal*.

The questionnaires were handed to the units by the researcher and collected again by the researcher. In order to prevent any difficulties during the process of the distribution of the questionnaires, an endorsement was obtained from the Turkish National Police (TNP) headquarters by the researcher.

*Toledo PD* To allow making comparisons, the same survey instrument was used in the Toledo Police Department in the summer of 2006. In total, 400 questionnaires were distributed via convenience sample in the Toledo Police Department, which has 799 staff, 686 of which are sworn officers. Of the 400 questionnaires, 296 were completed, yielding a response rate of 75%.

The Ohio Association of Chiefs of Police (OACP) has supported the study in Ohio. The OACP executive director made the initial contacts with the chief of the Toledo Police Department and asked for his support for the research. Later, the researcher met with the chief of police of the Toledo Police Department and the chief showed great interest in the study. The chief wrote a memo informing officers about an upcoming survey and encouraged all employees to complete the survey. The following week the surveys were distributed by the researcher. The research and planning bureau assisted the researcher in the data collection process. An officer from this bureau accompanied the researcher during the roll call visits in all the districts and divisions. The bureau made a schedule for three days, including visits to the three districts in the seven roll calls: 6:30 a.m., 7:30 a.m., 2:30 p.m., 3:30 p.m., 8:00 p.m., 10:30 p.m., and 11:30 p.m., respectively. On the fourth day, the administrative departments were visited. During the course of the survey, some officers were off that day or on vacation, and a few of them refused to take the survey.

At the roll calls, the shift supervisors informed the officers about the survey and introduced the researcher to the staff. The researcher presented brief information about the research goals, and kindly asked the officers to complete the survey. The researcher also offered TNP patches and KSU pens to the survey participants. The gifts were welcomed and highly appreciated by the officers. After the completion of the questionnaire, the respondents returned the survey instruments directly to the researcher.

The Toledo Police Department employees, from chief to the officer, showed great hospitality and assisted the researcher during the survey distribution. Being a police captain during that time in the TNP, the researcher felt as if he was at his home department in Turkey. This was a good advantage for the researcher, because he was treated like an insider, a fellow officer. The high response rate may be because of this circumstance.

There were several challenges to be addressed in interpreting the survey instrument for Toledo PD. The questionnaire was developed in Turkish, and administered in its original language in Ankara PD. Then, the questionnaire was translated by the author into English. After translating the survey, the instruments were submitted to a panel of experts for their review to ensure that the wording was clear and understandable.

For readability and interpretation of the items in the survey instruments, the draft questionnaire was given to several officers and supervisors at the KSU Police Department. Later, a pilot study was conducted in the Toledo Police Department to ensure comprehension and verify the readability of the survey instrument. The pilot group included all the ranking categories used in the final research project. Subjects from the two departments reviewed the instrument to ensure that the wording was compatible with terminology familiar to their employees. The commander of the planning and research section also made observations about the instruments, including comments that participants in the pilot study made to him. As a result of the pilot study, some items were rewritten and some items were added to clarify the instruments.

For example, in the draft questionnaire the following statement was used: "The completion of the performance evaluation forms of many personnel by the supervisor affects the credibility of the evaluation results." After the pilot study this statement was replaced by: "A supervisor's objectivity can be negatively affected by having to complete a large number of performance evaluations." As a second example, the statement "Performance evaluation system has no important contribution to the success of the organization" was replaced by "The current performance evaluation system makes no important contribution to the success of the organization" after the pilot study. The survey was revised according to the data received from all of these sources.

*Null Hypotheses*

**H1:** There will be no difference between Ankara and Toledo Police Departments' appraisal systems in regards to being closer to the best practices.

**H2:** There is no departmental difference with officers' perceptions regarding the *objectivity* of the appraisal system in their departments.

**H3:** There is no relationship between the rank of the officers and their perceptions regarding the *objectivity* of the appraisal system in their departments.

**H4:** There is no relationship between the education level of the officers and their perceptions regarding the *objectivity* of the appraisal system in their departments.

**H5:** There is no departmental difference with officers' perceptions regarding the *effectiveness* of the appraisal system in their departments.

**H6:** There is no relationship between the rank of the officers and their perceptions regarding the *effectiveness* of the appraisal system in their departments.

**H7:** There is no relationship between the education level of the officers and their perceptions regarding the *effectiveness* of the appraisal system in their departments.

*Analysis*

SPSS and STATA statistical software packages were used for the analyses. First, the frequency distributions for variables of interest, such as rank, age, years of service, education, and gender, are presented. Second, factor analysis was conducted for data reduction purposes. For instance, nine questions were reduced to two factors in Section 1. Third, bivariate and multiple regression models are used for hypotheses testing.

*Factor Analysis*

Factor analysis is a data reduction technique that groups variables on the basis of their intercorrelations (Kim & Mueller, 1989). The nine items regarding the officers' perceptions of their performance appraisal system in the questionnaire were factor analyzed to find out the items that had similar factors. In running the factor analysis, the principal components extraction technique was used, with orthogonal rotation of factors having eigenvalues of 1.0 or greater to a varimax solution. These factor analyses were performed separately on Ankara PD data, Toledo PD data, and on the combined data set. Table 5.1 presents loadings of variables on factors for Ankara PD, Toledo PD, and combined data, respectively.

Separate factor analyses for the Ankara and Toledo samples yielded very similar factor structures. As we examine the factor analysis results, it is clear that two interpretable factors were identified for analysis, although the two items' loading in Toledo PD data and one item's loading in both Ankara and Toledo data were relatively low. However, the rotated component matrix results for merged data revealed clearly two factors.

The principal component analysis using varimax rotation loaded nine items on two factors: a five-item objectivity factor and a four-item effectiveness factor. The five-item objectivity factor had a reliability of 0.755 (coefficient alpha) and explained 45% of the variance. This factor included the following five items: Performance evaluation reports do not differentiate between the successful and the unsuccessful employee; a supervisor's objectivity can be affected by the number of performance evaluations he or she completes; it is impossible to objectively evaluate the performance of the personnel with this system; personnel are not aware of the criteria used to evaluate them; and performance evaluations are negatively affected by factors such as friendship and personality traits. This factor represented the *objectivity* (fairness) of the appraisal system.

The second factor, which captures the dimension of effectiveness, was composed of four items: Annual/semiannual performance evaluations are a futile bureaucratic exercise; the current performance evaluation system does not accurately reflect an employee's abilities or work performance; the current performance evaluation system has no positive effect on the motivation of the personnel; and the current performance evaluation system makes no important contribution to the success of the organization. This factor represented the *effectiveness* (utility) of the appraisal system. The reliability of this factor was 0.789 and explained 12% of the variance.

**Table 5.1**  Factor Analysis Results (Rotated Component Matrix)

| QUESTIONNAIRE ITEM IMPORTANCE (WEIGHT) GIVEN TO: | ANKARA PD COMPONENT | | TOLEDO PD COMPONENT | | ANKARA-TOLEDO MERGED COMPONENT | |
|---|---|---|---|---|---|---|
| | 1 | 2 | 1 | 2 | 1 | 2 |
| 1 = Annual performance evaluations are a futile bureaucratic exercise | **0.609** | 0.404 | **0.549** | 0.357 | 0.451 | **0.546** |
| 2 = The current performance evaluation system does not accurately reflect an employee's abilities or work performance | **0.554** | 0.457 | **0.747** | 0.187 | 0.459 | **0.560** |
| 3 = The current performance evaluation system has no positive effect on the motivation of the personnel | **0.857** | 0.092 | **0.839** | 0.099 | 0.088 | **0.872** |
| 4 = The current performance evaluation system makes no important contribution to the success of the organization | **0.848** | 0.148 | **0.874** | 0.105 | 0.167 | **0.867** |
| 5 = Performance evaluation reports do not differentiate between the successful and the unsuccessful employee | 0.530 | **0.569** | **0.578** | 0.456 | **0.592** | 0.493 |
| 6 = A supervisor's objectivity can be affected by the number of performance evaluations he or she completes | 0.257 | **0.623** | 0.041 | **0.753** | **0.617** | 0.173 |
| 7 = It is impossible to objectively evaluate the performance of the personnel with this system | 0.452 | **0.626** | 0.458 | **0.415** | **0.674** | 0.312 |
| 8 = Personnel are not aware of the criteria used to evaluate them | 0.194 | **0.745** | 0.396 | **0.454** | **0.740** | 0.143 |
| 9 = Performance evaluations are negatively affected by factors such as friendship and personality traits | 0.028 | **0.783** | 0.182 | **0.760** | **0.672** | 0.081 |
| Cronbach alpha of the factors | 0.794 | 0.739 | 0.826 | 0.471 | **0.755** | **0.789** |

Extraction method: Principal component analysis.
Rotation method: Varimax with Kaiser normalization.

Given the clear factor loadings in the merged data, which eliminate any threat of intercolinearity, and the high alpha coefficients, which suggest strong internal consistency, the two factors should serve as valid measures.

*Regression Analysis*

Multiple regression is a statistical technique that is used to analyze the relationship between a single dependent variable and several independent variables (Tabachnick & Fidell, 2007). Therefore, in an effort to identify factors predictive of perceived objectivity and effectiveness of the performance appraisal system, multiple regression analyses were conducted.

Frequency distributions of the demographic characteristics are summarized for all variables, including rank, age, gender, educational level, years of service, assignment, and ethnicity. The mean and standard deviation were calculated for each item in the scales. After the regression analysis, postestimation tests for multicollinearity and heteroskedasticity were conducted, but neither problem was detected.

*Dependent Variables*

Based on the aforementioned factor analysis results, there are two dependent variables in this study: perceived *objectivity* and *effectiveness* of the appraisal system.

*Perceived Objectivity of the Appraisal System*    In order to measure police officers' and supervisors' perceived attitudes regarding the objectivity of the performance appraisal system, an index dependent variable is created based on the factor analysis results. As described above, the principal component analysis loaded five items under the objectivity factor. The dependent variable is made from these five items. These five items are summed to create the dependent variable titled "perceived objectivity of the appraisal system." Since the statements are negatively worded, and the Likert scale is from 1 = strongly disagree to 5 = strongly agree, *higher values mean a perception of a less objective appraisal system.* This variable has a range of 20 with a minimum value of 5 and a maximum value of 25. As we see from Figure 5.1, this variable is normally distributed.

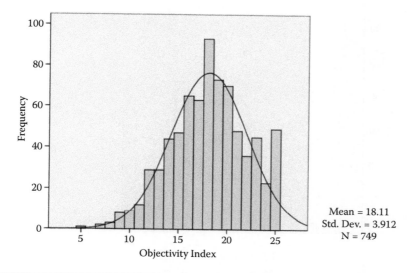

Mean = 18.11
Std. Dev. = 3.912
N = 749

**Figure 5.1** Histogram of the perceived objectivity of the appraisal system.

*Perceived Effectiveness of the Appraisal System*  In order to measure police officers' and supervisors' perceived attitudes regarding the effectiveness of the performance appraisal system, an index dependent variable is created based on the factor analysis results. As described above, the principal component analysis loaded four items under the effectiveness factor. These four items are summed to create our dependent variable titled "perceived effectiveness of the appraisal system." Again, since the statements are negatively worded, and the Likert scale is from 1 = strongly disagree to 5 = strongly agree, *higher values mean a perception of a less effective appraisal system.* This variable has a range of 16 with a minimum value of 4 and a maximum value of 20. As we see in Figure 5.2, this variable is normally distributed.

*Independent Variable*

There are three independent variables in this study: police department, rank, and education.

*Police Department*  This variable identifies whether the respondent is from the Ankara or Toledo Police Department. Ankara PD is coded as 1 and Toledo PD is coded as 0.

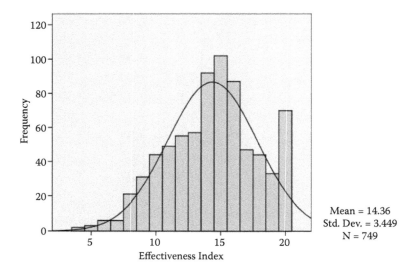

**Figure 5.2**   Histogram of perceived effectiveness of the appraisal system.

*Rank*   In order to test for the effect of rank on the dependent variables, the following question was used: "What is your current rank?" The response options for Ankara PD are: police officer, sergeant, lieutenant, captain, district captain, major, and chief. The rank structure in Toledo PD was as follows: police officer, sergeant, lieutenant, captain, and deputy chief.

In order to make the rank consistent with each department, rank variable was recoded in both data sets. In Ankara PD's data, district captains and captains were recoded as captains, and majors were recoded as chief since they serve as deputy chiefs in their departments in Ankara PD. Since there is one deputy chief in Toledo PD, it is recoded as chief in the merged data. Accordingly, a common rank structure that was applicable to each department was created. The following rank order was used in the combined data set: police officer, sergeant, lieutenant, captain, and chief.

*Education*   In order to test for the effect of education on the dependent variables, the following question was used: "What is your highest education completed?" The response options for Ankara PD were on an ordinal scale as follows: middle school, high school, police academy, BA degree, and graduate degree. For Toledo PD the answer options were: high school, some college, associate degree, BA degree, and graduate degree.

In order to make the education level consistent with each department, this variable was also recoded in both data sets. In Ankara PD's data, middle school and high school were recoded as 1 = high school or less. Since university and police academy have four years education and police academy is not necessarily higher or lower than college degree, they are combined and recoded as BA degree. In Toledo PD's data, some college, associate degree, and BA degree were recoded as 2 = some college to BA degree. Consequently, a common education level that was applicable to each department was created. The following education level was used in the combined data set: 1 = high school or less, 2 = some college to BA degree, and 3 = graduate degree.

*Control Variables*

The following variables are used as controls in the analysis: years of service, age, and gender. In order to be consistent with each department, some of the control variables that exist in the Toledo data, such as ethnicity and district information, but do not exist in Ankara data are excluded from the analyses. Age and years of service are likely to affect rank and education, and thus need to be used as controls to rule out possible spurious effect. Because we do not know what, if any, gender effect may emerge, gender is also included.

*Years of Service*  In order to control for the effect of years of service on the dependent variables, the following ordinal variable is used with the question: "What is your years of service?" The answer options for Ankara PD survey were 1–5 years, 6–10 years, 11–15 years, and 21 and up. However, in the Toledo PD survey instrument, the respondents were asked to enter their years of service on the questionnaire. Therefore, it was recoded in the same category as in the Ankara survey instrument.

*Age*  In order to control for the effect of age on the dependent variables, the following ordinal variable is used with the question: "What is your age?" The answer options for Ankara PD survey were 21–30,

31–40, 41–50, and 51 and up. Nevertheless, in the Toledo PD survey instrument, the respondents were asked to enter their age on the questionnaire. Hence, age was recoded in the same category as in the Ankara survey instrument.

*Gender*   In both Ankara PD and Toledo PD data gender was measured with a binary variable with male recoded as 0 and female recoded as 1.

The following section will report the findings of the analyses.

### Findings

This section tests the question of whether or not a performance appraisal system that fits more with the best practices creates greater satisfaction with the appraisal system. This study was designed to assess the reactions of officers and supervisors on the performance appraisal processes in Ankara and Toledo Police Departments. This study also tests whether there is a difference between Ankara and Toledo Police Department employees' perception of their performance appraisal system. The perceptions were examined through responses to identical surveys completed by officers and supervisors in the two police departments. Let's examine the findings of the analyses.

*Demographic Characteristics of the Survey Respondents in Ankara PD*

Table 5.2 reports the demographic characteristics of the survey respondents in Ankara PD. The survey sample includes 382 male officers (84.3%) and 70 female officers (15.5%). The majority of the respondents' ages are between 21 and 40 (68.3%). As for the education level of the participants, the majority is comprised of college graduates (53%). They are followed by the high school graduates (40.2%). Those with a graduate degree have a percentage of 3.5%.

As for the distribution according to the years of service, the subject's years of service are equally distributed over five-year increments (approximately each 20%). If the participants are examined according to the distribution of ranks, it is observed that 10.6% are police chiefs, 6.8% majors, 9.1% district captains, 9.5% captains, 10.4% lieutenants, 10.8% sergeants, and 42.8% police officers.

**Table 5.2** Demographic Characteristics of the Survey Respondents in Ankara PD

| VARIABLES | GROUPS | FREQUENCY | % |
|---|---|---|---|
| Gender | Female | 70 | 15.5 |
| | Male | 382 | 84.3 |
| | Missing | 1 | 0.2 |
| | **Total** | **453** | **100.0** |
| Age | 21–30 | 162 | 35.8 |
| | 31–40 | 147 | 32.5 |
| | 41–50 | 120 | 26.5 |
| | 51 and up | 21 | 4.6 |
| | Missing | 3 | 0.7 |
| | **Total** | **453** | **100.0** |
| Education | Middle school | 13 | 2.9 |
| | High school | 182 | 40.2 |
| | Collage (BA) | 240 | 53.0 |
| | Graduate school | 16 | 3.5 |
| | Missing | 2 | 0.4 |
| | **Total** | **453** | **100.0** |
| Years of service | 1–5 years | 99 | 21.9 |
| | 6–10 years | 91 | 20.1 |
| | 11–15 years | 82 | 18.1 |
| | 15–20 years | 88 | 19.4 |
| | 21 years and up | 87 | 19.2 |
| | Missing | 6 | 1.3 |
| | **Total** | **453** | **100.0** |
| Current rank | Police chief | 48 | 10.6 |
| | Major | 31 | 6.8 |
| | District captain | 41 | 9.1 |
| | Captain | 43 | 9.5 |
| | Lieutenant | 47 | 10.4 |
| | Sergeant | 49 | 10.8 |
| | Police officer | 194 | 42.8 |
| | **Total** | **453** | **100.0** |
| Supervisor/officer | Supervisor | 259 | 57.2 |
| | Officer | 194 | 42.8 |
| | **Total** | **453** | **100.0** |

About half of the sampling group has the rank of police officer (42.8%). However, if ranks other than the police officers are considered as supervisors, more than half of the group consists of the police supervisors (57.2%).

*Demographic Characteristics of the Survey Respondents in Toledo PD*

Table 5.3 reports the demographic characteristics of the survey respondents in Toledo PD. According to survey results, 81.4% (n = 241) of the respondents were male. The remaining 18.2% (n = 54) of the respondents were female. Regarding the age of the participants, the largest group (n = 98, 33.1%) was in the 31–40 years age group. The second largest group (n = 96, 32.4%) indicated their age as within the 41–50 years group. A very small proportion (n = 11, 3.7%) indicated that they were in the youngest age group of 21–30 years.

As for the education level of the participants, the largest group of respondents (n = 123, 41.6%) reported some college as their highest level of education. The next largest group (n = 77, 26%) indicated associate degree as their highest level of education. In addition, the majority of respondents (n = 223, 75.3%) indicated that their racial/ethnic origin was Caucasian/White. It was followed by African American (n = 40, 13.5%), and Hispanic (n = 22, 7.4%). Other ethnic groups were reported by very small numbers of the participants (1.7%).

The largest group of respondents (n = 98, 33.1%) indicated that they had been employed with their current department for greater than 21 years. Almost one-quarter (n = 66, 22.3%) of respondents indicated a tenure with the department of between 11 and 15 years. This was followed by 6–10 years (13.5%), 15–20 years (13.2%), and 1–5 years (9.1%), respectively.

The means and standard deviations for all variables are presented in Appendix B, and a correlation matrix of all variables is presented in Appendix C.

*Reactions to the Objectivity (Fairness) of the Appraisal System*

Table 5.4 examines the relationship between the respondent's department and his or her reactions to the objectivity of the appraisal system in his or her department.

The bivariate regression analysis above shows a positive relationship between Ankara PD and the objectivity of the appraisal system. Officers in Ankara PD perceive their appraisal system as more subjective than their counterparts in Toledo PD. Therefore, *we reject the null hypothesis* that there is no departmental difference with officers'

**Table 5.3** Demographic Characteristics of the Survey Respondents in Toledo PD

| VARIABLES | GROUPS | FREQUENCY | % |
|---|---|---|---|
| Gender | Female | 54 | 18.2 |
| | Male | 241 | 81.4 |
| | Missing | 1 | 0.3 |
| | **Total** | **295** | **99.7** |
| Age (M = 43.68) | 21–30 | 11 | 3.7 |
| | 31–40 | 98 | 33.1 |
| | 41–50 | 96 | 32.4 |
| | 51 and up | 67 | 22.6 |
| | Missing | 24 | 8.1 |
| | **Total** | **272** | **91.9** |
| Education | High school | 8 | 2.7 |
| | Some college | 123 | 41.6 |
| | Associates degree | 77 | 26.0 |
| | Bachelor degree | 67 | 22.6 |
| | Graduate school | 16 | 5.4 |
| | Missing | 5 | 1.7 |
| | **Total** | **291** | **98.3** |
| Years of service (M = 16.66) | 1–5 years | 27 | 9.1 |
| | 6–10 years | 40 | 13.5 |
| | 11–15 years | 66 | 22.3 |
| | 15–20 years | 39 | 13.2 |
| | 21 year and up | 98 | 33.1 |
| | Missing | 26 | 8.8 |
| | **Total** | **270** | **91.2** |
| Current rank | Police officer | 228 | 77 |
| | Sergeant | 38 | 12.8 |
| | Lieutenant | 22 | 7.4 |
| | Captain | 1 | 0.3 |
| | Deputy chief | 1 | 0.3 |
| | Missing | 6 | 2.0 |
| | **Total** | **290** | **98.0** |
| Current assignment | Operations | 206 | 69.6 |
| | Investigative | 49 | 16.6 |
| | Administrative | 38 | 12.8 |
| | Missing | 3 | 1.0 |
| | **Total** | **293** | **99.0** |

**(continued)**

**Table 5.3**  Demographic Characteristics of the Survey Respondents in Toledo PD (Continued)

| VARIABLES | GROUPS | FREQUENCY | % |
|---|---|---|---|
| Current district | Central | 146 | 49.3 |
| | North West | 58 | 19.6 |
| | Scott Park | 88 | 29.7 |
| | Missing | 4 | 1.4 |
| | **Total** | **292** | **98.6** |
| Ethnicity | White | 223 | 75.3 |
| | African American | 40 | 13.5 |
| | Hispanic | 22 | 7.4 |
| | Other | 5 | 1.7 |
| | Missing | 6 | 2 |
| | **Total** | **290** | **98.0** |

**Table 5.4**  Bivariate Analysis Between Departmental Differences and the Perceived Objectivity of the Appraisal System

| INDEPENDENT VARIABLE | B | STANDARD ERROR | P > T |
|---|---|---|---|
| **Ankara PD** | **1.567** | **0.275** | **0.000** |
| Constant | 17.165 | 0.194 | 0.000 |
| N | 749 | | |
| F | 0.000 | | |
| $R^2$ | 0.0384 | | |

perceptions regarding the *objectivity* of the appraisal system in their departments. This analysis reveals that Ankara PD officers perceive their appraisal system as less objective than the officers in Toledo PD.

Table 5.5 examines the relationship between the respondent's rank and his or her perceptions to the objectivity of the appraisal system in his or her department.

**Table 5.5**  Bivariate Analysis Between Rank and the Perceived Objectivity of the Appraisal System

| INDEPENDENT VARIABLE | B | STANDARD ERROR | P > T |
|---|---|---|---|
| **Rank** | **−0.213** | **0.108** | **0.049** |
| Constant | 18.569 | 0.245 | 0.000 |
| N | 743 | | |
| F | 0.048 | | |
| $R^2$ | 0.0062 | | |

**Table 5.6** Bivariate Analysis Between Education and the Perceived Objectivity of the Appraisal System

| INDEPENDENT VARIABLE | B | STANDARD ERROR | P > T |
|---|---|---|---|
| Education Constant | −0.412 | 0.296 | 0.165 |
| 18.842 | 0.558 | 0.000 | |
| N | 742 | | |
| F | 0.165 | | |
| R² | 0.0029 | | |

The bivariate regression analysis in Table 5.5 shows a negative relationship between the officer's rank and the objectivity of the appraisal system. This means that higher-ranking officers find the appraisal system less subjective compared to lower-ranking officers. Hence, *we reject the null hypothesis* that there is no relationship between the rank of the officers and their perceptions regarding the objectivity of the appraisal system in their departments. This finding reveals that higher-ranking officers in Ankara and Toledo Police Departments perceive their appraisal system as more objective than nonranking or lower-ranking officers.

Table 5.6 examines the relationship between the respondent's level of education and his or her perceptions regarding the objectivity of the appraisal system in his or her department.

The bivariate regression analysis results in Table 5.6 indicate that there is no statistically significant difference between the officer's level of education and his or her perceptions regarding the objectivity of the appraisal system. Thus, *we do not reject the null hypothesis* that there is no relationship between the education level of the officers and their perceptions regarding the *objectivity* of the appraisal system in their departments. This bivariate regression analysis reveals that an officer's education level does not affect his or her perceptions regarding the objectivity of the appraisal system.

Table 5.7 shows a multivariate regression analysis that examines the respondent's perceptions to the objectivity of the appraisal system in his or her departments

The multiple regression analysis results in Table 5.7 indicate that there is a statistically significant difference between Ankara PD and Toledo PD respondents' opinions regarding the objectivity of the

**Table 5.7**  Multivariate Analysis of the Perceived Objectivity of the Appraisal System[a]

| INDEPENDENT VARIABLES | B | STANDARD ERROR | P > T |
|---|---|---|---|
| **Ankara PD** | **2.934** | **0.478** | **0.000** |
| **Rank** | **−0.764** | **0.143** | **0.000** |
| **Education** | **1.318** | **0.373** | **0.000** |
| Male | −0.092 | 0.401 | 0.818 |
| Age | −0.196 | 0.302 | 0.516 |
| Years of service | 0.087 | 0.192 | 0.649 |
| N | 702 | | |
| F | 0.000 | | |
| R² | 0.088 | | |

Source:  The data were obtained from a survey of Ankara and Toledo Police Departments. Unstandardized regression coefficients, standard errors, and probabilities reported based on two-tailed test. Statistically significant coefficients are (p < 0.05) in bold. Ankara PD is coded as 1 and Toledo PD is coded as 0.
[a] The dependent variable is created based on factor analysis.

performance appraisal system. The direction of the relationship is positive. This means that Ankara PD staff perceive their appraisal process as being more subjective, compared to Toledo PD personnel. Consistent with the bivariate analysis finding, this multiple regression analysis reveals that officers in Ankara PD perceive their appraisal system as less objective than their colleagues in Toledo PD.

Another statistically significant relationship is found between the respondent's rank and his or her perceptions about the objectivity of his or her appraisal system. The direction of the relationship is negative. This means that as the rank increases the perception of subjectivity decreases. Consistent with the bivariate analysis finding, this multiple regression analysis reveals that higher-ranking officers find the appraisal system more objective than lower-ranking officers.

There is also a statistically significant relationship between police personnel's education level and their perceptions regarding the objectivity of the appraisal system. The direction of the relationship is positive. Officers who have higher-level education are more likely to be concerned with the subjectivity of the appraisal system. In other words, as the level of education increases, the officer's perception about the subjectivity of the appraisal system increases. In contrast to the bivariate analysis finding, this multiple regression analysis reveals education as a significant factor. This might be due to other variables in the model. Thus, this finding might not be reliable. However, having the education variable in the model is still valuable as a control variable.

There is no statistically significant relationship between the respondent's age, gender, years of service, and his or her opinions regarding the objectivity of the performance appraisal system. We are then able to rule out spurious effects in our main findings concerning rank and education.

### Reactions to the Effectiveness (Utility) of the Appraisal System

Table 5.8 examines the relationship between the respondent's department and his or her reactions to the effectiveness of the appraisal system in his or her department.

The bivariate regression analysis above shows no relationship between Ankara PD and the effectiveness of the appraisal system. Thus, *we do not reject the null hypothesis* that there is no departmental difference with officers' perceptions regarding the *effectiveness* of the appraisal system in their departments. This finding reveals that there is no statistically significant difference between the perceptions of Ankara and Toledo PD officers on the effectiveness of the appraisal system.

Table 5.9 examines the relationship between the respondents' rank and their reactions to the effectiveness of the appraisal system in their departments.

The bivariate regression analysis in Table 5.9 shows a negative relationship between the officer's rank and the effectiveness of the appraisal system. More specifically, higher-ranking officers find the appraisal system more effective than lower-ranking officers. Therefore, *we reject the null hypothesis* that there is no relationship between the rank of the officers and their perceptions regarding the *effectiveness* of

**Table 5.8**  Bivariate Analysis Between the Departmental Difference and the Perceived Effectiveness of the Appraisal System

| INDEPENDENT VARIABLE | B | STANDARD ERROR | P > T |
|---|---|---|---|
| Ankara PD | 0.099 | 0.258 | 0.702 |
| Constant | 14.300 | 0.200 | 0.000 |
| N | 749 | | |
| F | 0.7016 | | |
| $R^2$ | 0.00002 | | |

**Table 5.9** Bivariate Analysis Between Rank and the Perceived Effectiveness of the Appraisal System

| INDEPENDENT VARIABLE | B | STANDARD ERROR | P > T |
|---|---|---|---|
| **Rank** | −0.232 | **0.0874** | **0.008** |
| Constant | 14.846 | 0.221 | 0.000 |
| N | 743 | | |
| F | 0.008 | | |
| $R^2$ | 0.0095 | | |

**Table 5.10** Bivariate Analysis Between Education and the Perceived Effectiveness of the Appraisal System

| INDEPENDENT VARIABLE | B | STANDARD ERROR | P > T |
|---|---|---|---|
| Education | −0.101 | 0.246 | 0.682 |
| Constant | 14.542 | 0.454 | 0.000 |
| N | 742 | | |
| F | 0.682 | | |
| $R^2$ | 0.0002 | | |

the appraisal system in their departments. This finding reveals that higher-ranking officers find the appraisal system more effective than lower-ranking or nonranking officers.

Table 5.10 examines the relationship between the respondent's level of education and his or her reactions to the effectiveness of the appraisal system in his or her department.

The bivariate regression analysis results in Table 5.10 show no relationship between the officer's education level and his or her perceptions regarding the effectiveness of the appraisal system. Therefore, *we do not reject the null hypothesis* that there is no relationship between the education level of the officers and their perceptions regarding the *effectiveness* of the appraisal system in their departments. This bivariate regression analysis reveals that officers' education level does not affect their perceptions regarding the *effectiveness* of the appraisal system.

Table 5.11 examines respondents' reactions to the effectiveness of the appraisal system in their departments.

The multiple regression analysis results in Table 5.11 indicate that there is no statistically significant difference between the perceptions of the respondents from Ankara PD and Toledo PD on the

**Table 5.11** Multivariate Analysis of the Perceived Effectiveness of the Appraisal System[a]

| INDEPENDENT VARIABLES | B | STANDARD ERROR | P > T |
|---|---|---|---|
| Ankara PD | 0.496 | 436 | 256 |
| **Rank** | **−0.367** | **0.130** | **0.005** |
| Education | 0.428 | 0.340 | 0.208 |
| Male | 0.135 | 0.365 | 0.710 |
| Age | −0.332 | 0.275 | 0.228 |
| Years of service | 0.183 | 0.175 | 0.297 |
| N | 702 | | |
| F | 0.075 | | |
| $R^2$ | 0.016 | | |

*Source:* The data were obtained from a survey of Ankara and Toledo Police Departments. Unstandardized regression coefficients, standard errors, and probabilities reported based on two-tailed test. Statistically significant coefficients are ($p < 0.05$) in bold. Ankara PD is coded as 1 and Toledo PD is coded as 0.

[a] The dependent variable is created based on factor analysis.

effectiveness of the performance appraisal system. Consistent with the bivariate analysis, this multiple regression analysis reveals that there is no departmental difference with officers' perceptions regarding the *effectiveness* of the appraisal system in their departments.

However, there is a statistically significant difference between respondents' perception of the effectiveness of the appraisal system and their level of rank. The direction of the relationship is negative. This means that as the rank increases the perception of the appraisal system as being effective also increases. Consistent with the bivariate analysis, this multiple regression analysis reveals that higher-ranking officers in Ankara and Toledo Police Departments perceive their appraisal system as more *effective* than nonranking or lower-ranking officers.

There was no statistically significant relationship between other independent variables or the control variables and the opinions regarding the effectiveness of the performance appraisal system.

*Respondents' Attitudes on the Nature of Appraisal*

This section will report the findings (chi-square and descriptive statistics) of the Ankara and Toledo Police Department respondents' opinions about the sources of the appraisal (direct supervisor,

**Table 5.12**   Who Should Do the Performance Appraisal?

|  | ANKARA PD | | TOLEDO PD | |
| --- | --- | --- | --- | --- |
| CHOICES | FREQUENCY | % | FREQUENCY | % |
| Direct supervisor | 351 | 77.5 | 242 | 81.8 |
| Department chief | 24 | 5.3 | NA | NA |
| Peers | 36 | 7.9 | 28 | 9.5 |
| Self-evaluation | 8 | 1.8 | 5 | 1.7 |
| Missing | 34 | 7.5 | 21 | 7. |
| **Total** | **453** | **100** | **28** | **97.6** |

Chi-square value: 16.562, p = 0.001 (df = 3).

peers, etc.), frequency of the evaluation (six months, one year, etc.), and basis of the appraisal (job performance, personal characteristics, etc.).

### *Respondents' Attitudes on the Sources of the Appraisal*

Table 5.12 presents the respondents' opinions regarding who should do the performance appraisal. Based on chi-square statistics (p = 0.001), there is a significant difference between Ankara and Toledo PD officers' responses to the sources of appraisal.

When we examine the Ankara PD employees' responses, the majority of them (77.5%) believe that performance appraisal should be done by an immediate supervisor, followed by peers (7.9%), department chief (5.3%), and self-evaluation (1.8%). In the current appraisal system, department chiefs are the ones who conduct the evaluations. This finding indicates that officers are not happy with the existing format and they want the direct supervisor to perform the evaluation.

When we look at the Toledo PD officers' responses, we observe that most of the respondents (81.8%) would like the direct supervisor to do the appraisal. In Toledo PD's appraisal system, evaluations are conducted by the immediate supervisor. This finding indicates that the employees support the current format.

### *Respondents' Attitudes on the Frequency of the Appraisal*

Table 5.13 reports the respondents' opinions regarding the frequency of the performance appraisal. Based on chi-square statistics (p = 0.000),

Table 5.13    How Often Should the Performance Appraisals Be Done?

| | ANKARA PD | | TOLEDO PD | |
|---|---|---|---|---|
| CHOICES | FREQUENCY | % | FREQUENCY | % |
| Every 3 months | | | 14 | |
| Every 6 months | 80 | 17.7 | 112 | 4.7 |
| Once a year | 153 | 33.8 | 144 | 48.6 |
| Every 2 years | 9 | 2 | 10 | 5.4 |
| Missing | 4 | 0.9 | **295** | 3.3 |
| **Total** | **453** | **100** | | **99.7** |

Chi-square value: 31.345, p = 0.000 (df = 3).

there is a significant difference between Ankara and Toledo PD officers' responses to the frequency of the appraisal.

As can be seen from Table 5.13, the majority of the subjects (45.7%) in the Ankara PD sample believe that the evaluation should be done annually, and 33.8% consider that it should be done every 6 months. These responses show that the annual evaluation is the most desired evaluation.

The majority of the Toledo PD respondents (48.6%) also believe that the evaluations should be done once a year; 37.8% of them support the current frequency, which is twice a year. The majority of both police departments' respondents want to be evaluated once a year.

*Respondents' Attitudes on the Basis of the Appraisal*

Table 5.14 presents the respondents' opinions regarding the basis of the performance appraisal. Based on chi-square statistics (p = 0.000), there is a significant difference between Ankara and Toledo PD officers' responses to the basis of the appraisal.

Table 5.14    Which of the Following Should Be the Most Important Factor in Performance Appraisals?

| | ANKARA PD | | TOLEDO PD | |
|---|---|---|---|---|
| CHOICES | FREQUENCY | % | FREQUENCY | % |
| Job performance | 95 | 21 | 180 | 60.8 |
| Personal characteristics | 12 | 2.6 | 1 | 0.3 |
| All of the above | 337 | 74.4 | 112 | 37.8 |
| Missing | 9 | 2 | 3 | 1 |
| **Total** | **453** | **100** | **295** | **99.7** |

Chi-square value: 122.537, p = 0.000 (df = 2).

According to Table 5.14, 21% of the Ankara PD respondents believe that the most important factor in performance appraisal should be job performance, and 2.6% of them think that the main factor should be personal characteristics. A majority of the respondents (74.4%) wish that both job performance and personality characteristics could be considered in the evaluation.

A majority of the Toledo PD respondents (60.8%) think that only job performance should be taken into consideration during the evaluation; 37.8% of them believe that both job performance and personal characteristics should be evaluated.

# References

Bernardin, H. J., & Beatty, R. W. (1984). *Performance appraisal: Assessing human behavior at work.* Boston, MA: Kent Publishing Company.

Bernardin, H. J., Kane, J. S., Ross, S., Spina, D. S., & Johnson, D. L. (1995). Performance appraisal design, development, and implementation. In G. R. Ferris, S. D. Rosen, & D. T. Barnum (Eds.), *Handbook of human resource management* (pp. 462–493). Cambridge, MA: Blackwell.

Hughes, F. V. (1990). Performance appraisal systems in law enforcement. Unpublished doctoral dissertation, Michigan State University, Lansing, MI.

Ilgen, D. R. (1993). Performance appraisal accuracy: An illusive and sometimes misguided goal. In F. Landy, S. Zedeck, & J. Cleveland (Eds.), *Personnel selection and assessment: Individual and organizational perspectives.* Hillsdale, NJ: Lawrence Erlbaum, 235–252.

Jawahar, I. (2007). The influence of perceptions of fairness on performance appraisal reactions. *Journal of Labor Research, 28*(4), 735–754.

Keeping, L. M., & Levy, P. E. (2000). Performance appraisal reactions: Measurement, modeling, and method bias. *Journal of Applied Psychology, 85*(5), 708–723.

Kim, J., & Mueller, C. W. (1989). *Introduction to factor analysis: What it is and how to do it.* Newbury Park, CA: Sage Publications.

Latham, G. (1986). Job performance in appraisal. In C. L. Cooper & I. T. Robertson (Eds.), *International review of industrial and organizational psychology* (pp. 117–155). New York, NY: John Wiley & Sons.

Latham, G. P., Skarlicki, D., Irvine, D. & Siegel, J. P. (1993). The increasing importance of performance appraisals to employee effectiveness in organizational settings in North America. In C. L. Cooper & I. T. Robertson (Eds.), *International review of industrial and organizational psychology* (pp. 87–132). Chichester, UK: Wiley.

Murphy, K. R., & Cleveland, J. N. (1995). *Understanding performance appraisal: Social, organizational, and goal-oriented perspectives.* Newbury Park, CA: Sage.

Roberts, G. E. (1990). The influence of participation, goal setting, feedback and acceptance in measures of performance appraisal system effectiveness. Unpublished doctoral dissertation, University of Pittsburgh.

Schutt, R. (2006). *Investigating the social world: The process and practice of research.* Thousand Oaks, CA: Sage Publications.

Tabachnick, B. G., & Fidell, L. S. (2007). *Using multivariate analysis* (5th ed.). Boston, MA: Pearson/Allyn and Bacon.

# 6

## Conclusions

A primary goal of this book was to examine the performance appraisal systems of Ankara and Toledo Police Departments in order to explore the degree to which both police departments' performance appraisal systems include the factors that are recognized as important components of the performance appraisal process. This comparative case study allowed us to understand the similarities and differences between the two police department's appraisal systems in different organizational structures and cultures. As previously discussed, the case study analysis indicated that Toledo Police Department's appraisal system was closer to the best practices as described in the literature. Toledo PD's appraisal system included most of the key factors that are recognized as important components of the performance appraisal process in the literature. However, Ankara PD's appraisal system did not include most of the features of an effective appraisal system, and it was lacking very crucial components of a good appraisal system, such as feedback and rater training.

A second goal of this study was to assess the reactions of officers and supervisors regarding their performance appraisal process in Ankara and Toledo Police Departments. The perceptions were examined through responses to identical surveys completed by officers and supervisors in the two police departments. This allowed us to explore whether or not a performance appraisal system that more closely fits with the best practices creates greater satisfaction with the appraisal system. Employee reactions to performance appraisal have been suggested by researchers as being one of the components essential to the acceptance and use of performance appraisal in organizations (Bernardin & Beatty, 1984; Cardy & Dobbins, 1994; Murphy & Cleveland, 1995; Lilley & Hinduja, 2007). In addition, the effectiveness of an appraisal system is particularly contingent on the attitudes of the system users, both raters and ratees (Roberts, 1990).

Summary of the Research

In order to measure police officers' and supervisors' perceived attitudes regarding the performance appraisal system, two dependent variables (objectivity and effectiveness) were created based on the principal component analysis, which were considered to be indicators of employee satisfaction with the overall performance appraisal process. In an effort to identify factors predictive of *objectivity* and *effectiveness* of the performance appraisal system, bivariate and multiple regression analyses were conducted. In addition, the following independent and control variables were used in the analysis: department, rank, education, gender, age, and years of service.

This study tested whether there is a relationship between the departments, rank, education, gender, age, years of service, and officers' perceptions regarding the *objectivity* of the appraisal system. The findings revealed that officers in Ankara PD perceived their appraisal system as less objective than officers in Toledo PD. In other words, Ankara PD staffs perceive their appraisal process as being more subjective than Toledo PD personnel. This might be due to the fact that Ankara PD's appraisal system did not include most of the critical components of the best practices, such as feedback and rater training.

Similarly, Bobko, and Colella (1994), in their literature review of employee reactions to performance standards, concluded that clear, descriptive, and specific performance standards allow for feedback along with performance dimensions. They also argued that such performance standards would produce more desirable responses from employees. Indeed, several studies indicated that employees are more satisfied with appraisal systems that provide substantial feedback about job performance than with appraisal systems that provide little feedback (Dobbins, Cardy, & Platz-Vieno, 1990; Greller & Parsons, 1992). Additionally, employees tend to be more positive about performance appraisal systems in which the structure and the goal of the evaluation are well communicated and employees have active input into their own individual appraisals (Cawley, Keeping, & Levy, 1998; Narcisse & Harcourt, 2008; Kavanagh, Benson, & Brown, 2007; Mamatoglu, 2008).

Surveying a total of 629 people in a research and development organization, Dipboye and de Pontbriand (1981) found that employees held a more positive attitude toward their appraisal system when they had an opportunity to state their own opinions, and when they had the opportunity to discuss objectives and plans. However, the respondents did not like the idea of being evaluated based on criteria that are not related to their job. Our findings are also in parallel with this literature. Since Ankara PD has characteristic-based evaluation criteria in its appraisal system, personnel were dissatisfied with the system. It was opposite in Toledo PD. The appraisal system has job-relevant criteria, so the employees are happier with such a behavioral-based, job-relevant evaluation. Regression analyses support these arguments.

There was also a negative significant relationship between the respondents' rank and their perceptions regarding the objectivity of their appraisal system. Regardless of the officers' departments, as the ranks increased their perception of subjectivity decreased. In other words, higher-ranking officers saw the appraisal system as being more objective than did lower-ranking officers. This finding is parallel with the literature. For instance, Williams and Levy (2000) found that supervisors reported significantly higher levels of satisfaction with performance evaluation than did nonsupervisory employees. According to them, this finding was due to supervisors being more exposed to the process and better trained. Thus they have more information to assess the system. In our example, higher-ranking officers see the appraisal system as more objective than lower-ranking officers, perhaps because they want to keep the status quo and not give up their control powers. Why the higher-ranking officers have a better perception of the effectiveness of the appraisal system in their departments is beyond the scope of this research and future studies should address this question.

In the multiple regression analyses, officers' education level emerged as another statistically significant factor in determining the views toward the objectivity of the appraisal system. Officers from both departments who have higher levels of education are more likely to be concerned with the subjectivity of the appraisal system than those who have lower levels of education. Put differently, as the level of education increases, the officer's perception about the subjectivity of the appraisal system also increases. This finding suggests a possible significance of education in law enforcement and its possible importance for organizational development. If an organization can increase the overall quality of its personnel through employing better-educated staff or providing opportunities for its personnel to increase their educational level, it may produce better products and services. It may be because better-educated employees can see the deficiencies and problems easier and contribute to the overall quality in the organization. However, the results related to education in the regression analysis should be accepted with caution because education was not significant in the bivariate analyses. It is not clear why education emerges as significant in the regression but not in the bivariate analysis. Perhaps when including rank, gender, age, and years of service, education then emerges. But these results are not clear, so they must be accepted with caution.

There was no statistically significant relationship between the respondents' age, gender, years of service, and their opinions regarding the objectivity of the performance appraisal system. Thus we are able to rule out spurious effects of age, gender, and years of service on the hypothesized relations concerning rank and education.

This research also tested whether there is a relationship between the departments, rank, education, gender, age, years of service, and officers' perceptions regarding the *effectiveness* of the appraisal system. The findings showed no statistically significant difference between the perceptions of the respondents from Ankara PD and Toledo PD on the effectiveness of the performance appraisal system of their respective department. In other words, there was no difference between the two departments in terms of the personnel's opinions on effectiveness of the performance appraisal system in their departments. This finding means that the opinion of the police personnel on the effectiveness of the performance appraisal system is not something that varies across different organizational structures or cultures. Since we could not find any statistically significant relationship between the effectiveness of the system and education, department, age, years of service, and gender, these variables do not explain the officers' perception of the effectiveness of the appraisal system in their departments.

However, rank was a significant factor. As the rank of the officers increases, their perception of the appraisal system effectiveness also increases. In other words, higher-ranking officers find the appraisal system more effective than lower-ranking officers. This finding is consistent with Gul, Dogutas, and Dolu's (2010) study that district captains and captains are less concerned with the secret appraisal system than police officers. This might be due to the fact that it is the supervisors who are responsible for the system. Being supervisors, they will of course see the system as running effectively and flawlessly since its effectiveness is a reflection of their performance.

This study also examined the survey respondent's opinion regarding the nature of the appraisal. In terms of the *sources of the appraisal*, the findings revealed that most of the employees in both Toledo PD (81.8%) and Ankara PD (77.5%) preferred that the immediate supervisor do the appraisal. In Toledo PD's appraisal system, evaluations are conducted by the immediate supervisor, whereas in Ankara PD, it is the department chiefs who conduct the evaluations in the current appraisal system. This finding indicates that the officers of Toledo PD support the current format, while their colleagues in Ankara PD are not pleased with the existing system. Officers of Ankara PD would like to see their direct supervisor perform the evaluation.

Supervisors who have sufficient job knowledge and access to the employee should be the raters (Roberts, 1998). Managers in the TNP should delegate the task of conducting the performance appraisal to the immediate supervisor. Evaluation must be completed by someone who has the most knowledge about the employees' work, their everyday routines, and the strengths and weaknesses of their job performance. Therefore, evaluations by higher administrators, such as the department chief in the Ankara PD example, may yield ineffective and perhaps unreliable results. In fact, most of the time department chiefs are not familiar with the officers' performance, and sometimes they have too many officers to supervise. They cannot know the employees well enough to do a valid and reliable evaluation.

In terms of the *frequency of the performance appraisal*, again, a large majority of the subjects in Toledo PD (48.6%) and Ankara PD (45.7%) believe that the evaluation should be done annually. The Toledo PD employees are currently evaluated twice a year. This finding indicates that most of the respondents in Toledo PD, like their counterparts in Ankara PD, would prefer an annual evaluation. Even though annual evaluation is a common practice (Murphy & Cleveland, 1995), performance appraisal should be an ongoing process rather than an event (Bernardin & Beatty, 1984).

When we examined respondents' opinions regarding the *basis of the performance appraisal*, the findings revealed that a majority of the respondents (74.4%) in Ankara PD wanted both job performance and personality characteristics to be considered in the evaluation. On the other hand, a majority of the Toledo PD respondents (60.8%) think that only job performance should be taken into consideration during the evaluation. Opinions of officers from Ankara PD on personal characteristics might be an outcome of cultural setting and their past experiences.

Ratings based on personality characteristics have no support in current literature (Latham & Wexley, 1994; Varma, DeNisi, & Peters, 1996). Studies have indicated that behaviorally based methods exhibit a significant improvement in reliability and validity over characteristic-based systems (Tziner, Kopelman, & Joanis, 1997). In addition, this approach gets away from measuring subjective personal characteristics and instead measures observable, critical behaviors that are related to specific job dimensions (Bopp & Whisenand, 1980).

This study revealed that Toledo Police Department's appraisal system is closer to the best practices, which in turn was perceived as more objective by their employees. In previous research, appraisal orientation toward professional growth and development was associated with satisfaction (Cawley et al., 1998). According to Roberts and Reed's (1996) study, employees who viewed the appraisal process as developmental in nature demonstrated more participation and cooperation. Rater training was also linked with employee satisfaction with the appraisal system (Wanguri, 1995; Spears & Parker, 2002). There was evidence that employee development and coaching skills could be improved through rater training (Roberts & Reed, 1996). Lilley and Hinduja's (2007) study also revealed that the police departments that provided more training to raters, utilized a variety of performance criteria, and used the performance appraisal for officer development were more satisfied with their evaluation system than other departments.

Therefore, the higher satisfaction level of the officers with regard to their appraisal system might be explained by the Toledo Police Department's having most of the features of the best practices, such as developmental goal and rater training.

The failure of the Ankara Police Department to implement sound, well-established performance appraisal practices may have negative consequences for the individual employee. Since the TNP has a highly centralized structure and gives a lot of power to the supervisors, the police performance appraisal system in TNP serves to promote the organizational status quo, thereby hindering the ability of the department to align its strategies with the contemporary systems. In Ankara PD's appraisal system, there is only feedback if the evaluation is highly negative, which is very rare. There is no way employees can challenge what they may perceive to be an unfair or biased evaluation from their supervisors. This obviously leads to a situation where employees are forced to accept whatever evaluation decisions management makes about their work status.

In light of the fact that findings are based on a sample of Ankara and Toledo Police Departments, one might want to question to what extent these results are generalizable to other police organizations. It is conceivable that the results do not generalize to all settings. The survey sample in the TNP only included employees of the Ankara PD. Considering that TNP is a very large law enforcement agency with its central office and 81 provincial departments, it was difficult to select among many alternatives. However, we preferred Ankara as an initial step to explore what the personnel in the police organization in Turkey think about the performance appraisal system in TNP. Indeed, this study can be replicated in other provincial departments or in central departments, but we believe that the results will be pretty much the same because of the uniformity of the system across the country.

One might also want to question the different time periods when the surveys were conducted: 2001 in Ankara and 2006 in Toledo. It is important to note, however, that no significant alteration was made to the TNP's performance appraisal system until quite recently (i.e., 2011). So, one can certainly argue that these findings are still valid and true today. Thus, a survey conducted in Ankara during 2006 would not have yielded different results. Nevertheless, one might consider replicating this study by adding new questions, such as the unit of the respondent, service branch of the respondent, and so forth.

Another limitation of this study might be the negative wording of the survey questionnaire. One can argue that in the original survey instrument used in Ankara PD, the statements were negatively worded.

However, we had to use the same survey in Toledo PD in order to maintain the consistency between the two surveys. Future studies can take a more positive stand in setting up the questionnaire instrument.

Consequently, this study suggests that departmental differences, rank, and education are the significant factors that determine the officers' perception of the objectivity of the appraisal system in their departments, whereas gender, years of service, and age do not matter. However, when the study focus was on the effectiveness of the system, officer perceptions toward the effectiveness of the appraisal system only changed as the ranks of the officers changed. Higher-ranking officers held a more positive view of the effectiveness of the appraisal system in their departments. Departmental differences, education, gender, years of service, and age did not matter.

In light of the findings of this research, if we want to increase the effectiveness of the system as seen by the officers, we need to find out why lower-ranking and nonranking officers see their appraisal system as less effective than do the ranking officers. Similarly, if we want to increase the objectivity of the system, we should find out why departmental differences made a difference in reflecting different perceptions regarding the objectivity of the appraisal systems in both police departments. Why officers from Toledo PD had a better view of the objectivity of the appraisal system in their department and why those in Ankara PD had a more negative view should be examined closely. Such differences might stem from the organizational, policing philosophy, or cultural differences in these departments. As discussed before, since Toledo PD had most of the characteristics of the best practices in performance appraisal, the officers from Toledo PD had a better view of the system in their department.

The findings of this study also suggest that the more an appraisal system gains the features of the best practices in performance appraisal, not only might it be more effective, but also the employees might find the system to be fair and objective. Thus it is important to have an appraisal system that includes critical components of the best practices.

Based on the literature review and our research, we offer the following items of an appraisal system, which should necessarily be contained in police performance appraisal systems:

## Essential Features of an Effective Appraisal System

- Objective and clear descriptions of duties and responsibilities for all positions. These 'job descriptions' must be published and understood by all parties.
- Individual performance goals that are be set in advance for all employees. Raters and ratees should have input into the development of these goals.
- Individual performance goals that are logically linked to unit and department performance goals.
- Performance ratings that are "data based." That is, evaluations should be based upon objective performance data such as attendance records, arrest and summons activity, discipline records, etc. Subjective assessments alone are not sufficient.
- A substantive and collaborative post-evaluation meeting between rater and rate.
- An opportunity for ratees to provide input (perhaps even to appraise their own performance) and to discuss the substance of the evaluation with the rater in the post-evaluation interview.
- A system for recording the discussions that take place during the post-evaluation interview.
- Clarity with regard to the exact process for dealing with "unsatisfactory" appraisals. Any re-training or additional supervision should be clearly articulated.
- The performance appraisal process must be linked to the department's internal discipline system (for officers deemed to have performed poorly) and to the department's internal 'rewards' system (for those who have distinguished themselves through superior performance). Although it is not possible to financially reward officers for superior performance, it should be possible to link superior performance to additional training, promotion and/or desired or "special" assignments. All police organizations should have either an express or understood "career path" for individuals who wish to move upwards through the ranks.
- A well-defined process for appealing an evaluation, and for reviewing it at a higher level of supervision.

- Distinct evaluation criteria for personnel performing different duties. A "one –size-fits-all" evaluation for all personnel at a particular rank (e.g., for all police officers, whether they perform patrol duties, crime analysis, field training and supervision, etc.) is not recommended.
- The evaluations themselves must be descriptive and must include narrative responses (listing particular examples), as opposed to "fill-in-the-blank" forms.
- Proper and continuing training and support for raters.

In order to be effective, any personal performance appraisal system absolutely must be linked to a department's: stated organizational mission; recruit (i.e., police academy) training; orientation; field training; in-service training; promotional standards and procedures; and official recognition and rewards program.

We believe that a well-designed and well-executed performance appraisal system of any given police or other public organization that includes these features might have a greater efficiency, effectiveness, and improved employee morale.

In considering future revisions and improvements of the performance appraisal systems in Toledo and Ankara Police Departments, and as well as in other police departments, the findings of this study should produce some insights to provide guidance to future efforts to design better appraisal systems. Insights from this study may also contribute to nationwide assessments of evaluation practices and standards for the police organizations.

### Recommendations for Future Research

Future research should try to replicate the validity of these findings in different police agencies with diverse characteristics.

This research showed that conducting a pilot study is helpful before distributing the surveys. It is very important to make sure that the target population understands what the researcher means. This is especially crucial in cross-national and cross-cultural studies.

Future research should take into account the limitations of this study and should avoid such limitations.

Future research should examine closely the factors that might lead officers to have a negative perception of the objectivity of the performance appraisal system in their departments. Such factors might include departmental subculture, organizational differences, national and cultural differences, and alike.

Future research should also consider what might be causing the relationship between rank and satisfaction with appraisal systems. In other words, why higher-ranking officers have a better perception of the effectiveness of the appraisal system in their departments is a question worth exploring.

## Conclusion

This book has attempted to address a variety of complex issues that are associated with the development, structure, and operation of police performance evaluation programs. We have identified certain essential features that both promote and restrict the operation of such performance evaluation systems. Even the best-designed systems are likely to fail if they are not properly supported by well-trained managers and well-meaning employees who sincerely wish to enhance both their personal performance levels and the performance of the entire organization. Our detailed comparison of the evaluation systems of both the TNP and the Toledo, Ohio, Police Department reveals that two very distinct systems can nevertheless share some interesting similarities. Police managers should look to these systems, as well as others, in an effort to personally identify best practices in the field.

Like any other performance management system, these programs cannot be imposed upon a police organization. Rather, they must be developed from within, by employers and employee stakeholders, and they must conform to and build upon each department's particular history and organizational culture. All levels of the organization must be actively involved.

We are confident that thoughtful police managers will continue to use annual performance reviews correctly "to hold people accountable for the commitments they make to the other members of the organization" (Stack, 1997, p. 39). They will also need to work intelligently to incorporate performance management techniques throughout the entire year and to make significant improvements upon existing police performance evaluation systems when necessary. Just as with any other business or human enterprise, the assessment of performance (even just informally) must be a continuous process and must be viewed as a responsibility, not as a necessary evil.

In the years to come, the ever-increasing demand for accountability and continuous improvement will ensure that all police agencies will expend considerable time, thought, and resources to the development and use of fair, accurate and effective personal performance appraisal systems. We hope that this text will assist, in some small way, in that endeavor.

# References

Bernardin, H. J., & Beatty, R. W. (1984). *Performance appraisal: Assessing human behavior at work.* Boston, MA: Kent Publishing Company.

Bobko, P., & Colella, A. (1994). Employee reactions to performance standards: A review and research propositions. *Personnel Psychology, 47*(1), 1–29.

Bopp, W., & Whisenand, P. (1980). *Police personnel administration* (2nd ed.). Boston, MA: Allyn and Bacon.

Cardy, R. L., & Dobbins, G. H. (1994). *Performance appraisal: Alternative perspectives.* Cincinnati, OH: South-Western.

Cawley, B., Keeping, L., & Levy, P. (1998). Participation in the performance appraisal process and employee reactions: A meta analytic review of field investigations. *Journal of Applied Psychology, 83*(4), 615–633.

Dipboye, R. L., & de Pontbriand, R. (1981). Correlates of employee reactions to performance appraisals and appraisal systems. *Journal of Applied Psychology, 66*(2), 248–251.

Dobbins, G. H., Cardy, R. L., & Platz-Vieno, S. J. (1990). A contingency approach to appraisal satisfaction: An initial investigation of the joint effects of organizational variables and appraisal characteristics. *Journal of Management, 16*(3), 619–632.

Greller, M. M., & Parsons, C. K. (1992). Feedback and feedback inconsistency as sources of strain and self evaluation. *Human Relations, 45*, 601–620.

Gul, S. K., O. Dolu, & C. Dogutas. (2010). Performance Appraisal System in the Turkish National Police: The Case of Ankara Police Department. *Police Practice and Research: An International Journal,* 11(6), 505-519.

Kavanagh, P., Benson, J., & Brown, M. (2007). Understanding performance appraisal fairness. *Asia Pacific Journal of Human Resources, 45*(2), 132–150.

Latham, G. P., & Wexley, K. N. (1994). *Increasing productivity through performance appraisal.* Reading, MA: Addison-Wesley.

Lilley, D., & Hinduja, S. (2007). Police officer performance appraisal and overall satisfaction. *Journal of Criminal Justice, 35*, 137–150.

Mamatoglu, N. (2008). Effects on organizational context (culture and climate) from implementing a 360-degree feedback system: The case of Arcelik. *European Journal of Work and Organizational Psychology, 17*(4), 426–449.

Murphy, K. R., & Cleveland, J. N. (1995). *Understanding performance appraisal: Social, organizational, and goal-oriented perspectives.* Newbury Park, CA: Sage.

Narcisse, S., & Harcourt, M. (2008). Employee fairness perceptions of performance appraisal: A Saint Lucian case study. *International Journal of Human Resource Management, 19*(6), 1152–1169.

Roberts, G. E. (1990). The influence of participation, goal setting, feedback and acceptance in measures of performance appraisal system effectiveness. Unpublished doctoral dissertation, University of Pittsburgh.

Roberts, G. E. (1998). Perspectives in enduring and emerging issues in performance appraisal. *Public Personnel Management, 27*(3), 301–320.

Roberts, G., & Reed, T. (1996). Performance appraisal participation, goal setting and feedback: The influence of supervisory style. *Review of Public Administration, 16*, 29–60.

Spears, M., & Parker, D. (2002). A probit analysis of the impact of training on performance appraisal satisfaction. *American Business Review, 20*, 12–16.

Tziner, A., Kopelman, R., & Joanis, C. (1997). Investigation of raters' and ratees' reactions to three methods of performance appraisal: BOS, BARS, and GRS. *Revue Canadienne des Sciences de l'Administration, 14*, 396–404.

Varma, A., DeNisi, A. S., & Peters, L. H. (1996). Interpersonal affect and performance appraisal: A field study. *Personnel Psychology, 49*(2), 341–360.

Wanguri, D. (1995). A review, an integration, and a critique of cross-disciplinary research on performance appraisals, evaluations, and feedback: 1980–1990. *Journal of Business Communications, 32*(3), 267–272.

Williams, J. R., & Levy, P. E. (2000). Investigating some neglected criteria: The influence of organizational level and perceived system knowledge on appraisal reactions. *Journal of Business and Psychology, 14*(3), 501–513.

# Appendix A
# Survey Instrument

■                                                             ■

## Toledo Police Department
## Performance Evaluation Survey

**MARKING INSTRUCTIONS**
- Use a No. 2 pencil or a blue or black ink pen only.
- Do not use pens with ink that soaks through the paper.
- Make solid marks that fill the response completely.
- Make no stray marks on this form.

CORRECT: ●      INCORRECT: ⊘ ⊠ ⊖ ☉

### I. Opinions Regarding the Existing Performance Evaluation System

| | Strongly Disagree | Disagree | Neutral | Agree | Strongly Agree |
|---|---|---|---|---|---|
| 1. Semi-annual performance evaluations are a futile bureaucratic exercise. | ○ | ○ | ○ | ○ | ○ |
| 2. The current performance evaluation system does not accurately reflect an employee's abilities or work performance. | ○ | ○ | ○ | ○ | ○ |
| 3. The current performance evaluation system has no positive effect on the motivation of the personnel. | ○ | ○ | ○ | ○ | ○ |
| 4. The current performance evaluation system makes no important contribution to the success of the organization. | ○ | ○ | ○ | ○ | ○ |
| 5. Performance evaluation reports do not differentiate between the successful and the unsuccessful employee. | ○ | ○ | ○ | ○ | ○ |
| 6. A supervisor's objectivity can be negatively affected by having to complete a large number of performance evaluations. | ○ | ○ | ○ | ○ | ○ |
| 7. Using a computer program for performance evaluation is helpful. | ○ | ○ | ○ | ○ | ○ |
| 8. It is impossible to objectively evaluate the performance of the personnel with this system. | ○ | ○ | ○ | ○ | ○ |
| 9. Personnel are not aware of the criteria used to evaluate them. | ○ | ○ | ○ | ○ | ○ |
| 10. Performance evaluations are negatively affected by factors such as friendship and personality traits. | ○ | ○ | ○ | ○ | ○ |

### II. Opinions on Creating a Contemporary Performance Evaluation System

| | Strongly Disagree | Disagree | Neutral | Agree | Strongly Agree |
|---|---|---|---|---|---|
| 1. In order to design an evaluation system based on objective criteria, clear job descriptions and job task analyses have to be in place. | ○ | ○ | ○ | ○ | ○ |
| 2. Knowing the evaluation criteria affects the employee's overall performance. | ○ | ○ | ○ | ○ | ○ |
| 3. The performance evaluation results should be passed on to the employee by the supervisor in an individual meeting. | ○ | ○ | ○ | ○ | ○ |
| 4. Both positive and negative recognition of the employee should be taken into consideration in the evaluation. | ○ | ○ | ○ | ○ | ○ |
| 5. Additional training that personnel receive during the evaluation period should be taken into consideration. | ○ | ○ | ○ | ○ | ○ |
| 6. Performance evaluation questions should be stated clearly. | ○ | ○ | ○ | ○ | ○ |
| 7. Performance evaluation results should be used as a criterion in rewarding personnel. | ○ | ○ | ○ | ○ | ○ |
| 8. The performance evaluation results should assist in determining personnel's in-service training and improvement needs. | ○ | ○ | ○ | ○ | ○ |
| 9. Performance evaluation results should be used in administrative decisions (appointment, promotion, etc.) | ○ | ○ | ○ | ○ | ○ |
| 10. The performance evaluation results should be used in determining the salary increase of personnel. | ○ | ○ | ○ | ○ | ○ |
| 11. Training programs for supervisors about performance evaluation contributes to a more effective and objective evaluation. | ○ | ○ | ○ | ○ | ○ |
| 12. The police organization should have a unique performance evaluation system particular to its own structure and service nature. | ○ | ○ | ○ | ○ | ○ |

■     ■

**13.** Which of the following should be the most important factor in performance evaluations?

○ Job performance    ○ Personality traits    ○ Both of them    ○ Other: _____

**14.** Who should do the performance evaluation?

○ Direct Supervisor    ○ Peers    ○ Other: _____
○ Department Chief    ○ Self Evaluation

**15.** How often should the performance evaluations be done?

○ Every 3 months    ○ Once a year    ○ Other: _____
○ Every 6 months    ○ Every 2 years

### III. Demographics

(This information will be kept strictly confidential and is collected for statistical purposes only.)

**1.** Current Rank                       **2.** Years of Service:

○ Police Officer    ○ Captain
○ Lieutenant    ○ Sergeant
○ Detective    ○ Deputy Chief

**3.** Current assignment

○ Vice/Metro    ○ Invesitgative Services
○ Gangs    ○ Directed Patrol
○ Operations    ○ Other: _____
○ Administrative _____

**4.** Please specify your district:

○ Central    ○ Northwest    ○ Scott Park

**5.** Gender: ○ Male ○ Female                **6.** Age:

**7.** Ethnicity: (**mark all that apply**)

○ Caucasian    ○ Asian American
○ Hispanic    ○ Mixed Ethnicity
○ African American    ○ Other: _____
○ Native American _____

**8.** Highest Education:

○ High School    ○ Bachelor Degree    ○ Associate Degree
○ Some College    ○ Graduate Degree

**9.** If you have any additional comments, please write below or on the back of the sheet.

_____

_____

_____

# Appendix B
# Descriptive Statistics of the Variables

| VARIABLES | N | MEAN | STANDARD DEVIATION | MINIMUM | MAXIMUM | RANGE |
|---|---|---|---|---|---|---|
| Objectivity index | 749 | 18.11 | 3.912 | 5 | 25 | 20 |
| Performance evaluation reports do not differentiate between the successful and the unsuccessful employee | 748 | 3.58 | 1.141 | 1 | 5 | 4 |
| A supervisor's objectivity can be affected by the number of performance evaluations he or she completes | 747 | 3.76 | 1.018 | 1 | 5 | 4 |
| It is impossible to objectively evaluate the performance of the personnel with this system | 747 | 3.60 | 1.069 | 1 | 5 | 4 |
| Personnel are not aware of the criteria used to evaluate them | 747 | 3.53 | 1.151 | 1 | 5 | 4 |
| Performance evaluations are negatively affected by factors such as friendship and personality traits | 749 | 3.65 | 1.108 | 1 | 5 | 4 |
| Effectiveness index | 749 | 14.36 | 3.449 | 4 | 20 | 16 |

(continued)

**145**

| VARIABLES | N | MEAN | STANDARD DEVIATION | MINIMUM | MAXIMUM | RANGE |
|---|---|---|---|---|---|---|
| Annual/semiannual performance evaluations are a futile bureaucratic exercise | 749 | 3.41 | 1.130 | 1 | 5 | 4 |
| The current performance evaluation system does not accurately reflect an employee's abilities or work performance | 747 | 3.91 | 0.963 | 1 | 5 | 4 |
| The current performance evaluation system has no positive effect on the motivation of the personnel | 748 | 3.52 | 1.171 | 1 | 5 | 4 |
| The current performance evaluation system makes no important contribution to the success of the organization | 746 | 3.55 | 1.128 | 1 | 5 | 4 |
| Ankara PD | 749 | 0.60 | 0.489 | 0 | 1 | 1 |
| Rank | 743 | 2.08 | 1.444 | 1 | 5 | 4 |
| Education | 742 | 1.77 | 0.514 | 1 | 3 | 2 |
| Male | 747 | 0.83 | 0.372 | 0 | 1 | 1 |
| Age | 722 | 2.30 | 0.967 | 1 | 4 | 3 |
| Years of service | 717 | 3.16 | 1.440 | 1 | 5 | 4 |

# Appendix C
## Correlation Matrix for All the Variables

|  |  | OBJECTIVITY INDEX | EFFECTIVENESS INDEX | ANKARA PD | RANK | EDUCATION | MALE | AGE | YEARS OF SERVICE |
|---|---|---|---|---|---|---|---|---|---|
| Objectivity Index | Pearson correlation | 1 | 0.621(**) | 0.196(**) | -0.079(*) | -0.054 | -0.041 | -0.178(**) | -0.145(**) |
|  | Significance (two-tailed) |  | 0.000 | 0.000 | 0.032 | 0.141 | 0.265 | 0.000 | 0.000 |
|  | Sum of squares and cross-products | 11,447.354 | 6,266.359 | 280.591 | -330.211 | -80.642 | -44.392 | -488.916 | -589.285 |
|  | Covariance | 15.304 | 8.377 | 0.375 | -0.445 | -0.109 | -0.060 | -0.678 | -0.823 |
|  | N | 749 | 749 | 749 | 743 | 742 | 747 | 722 | 717 |
| Effectiveness Index | Pearson correlation | 0.621(**) | 1 | 0.196(**) | -0.097(**) | -0.015 | -0.016 | -0.057 | -0.044 |
|  | Significance (two-tailed) | 0.000 |  | 0.014 | 0.008 | 0.682 | 0.659 | 0.127 | 0.240 |
|  | Sum of squares and cross-products | 6,266.359 | 8,898.670 | 17.702 | -359.713 | -19.776 | -15.513 | -137.111 | -156.247 |
|  | Covariance | 8.377 | 11.897 | 0.024 | -0.485 | -0.027 | -0.021 | -0.190 | -0.218 |
|  | N | 749 | 749 | 749 | 743 | 742 | 747 | 722 | 717 |
| Ankara PD | Pearson correlation | 0.196(**) | 0.014 | 1 | 0.427(**) | -0.404(**) | 0.037 | -0.404(**) | -0.196(**) |
|  | Significance (two-tailed) | 0.000 | 0.702 |  | 0.000 | 0.000 | 0.312 | 0.000 | 0.000 |
|  | Sum of squares and cross-products | 280.591 | 17.702 | 179.023 | 223.248 | -75.063 | 5.031 | -136.496 | -98.071 |
|  | Covariance | 0.375 | 0.024 | 0.239 | 0.301 | -0.101 | 0.007 | -0.189 | -0.137 |
|  | N | 749 | 749 | 749 | 743 | 742 | 747 | 722 | 717 |

| | | | | | | | | | |
|---|---|---|---|---|---|---|---|---|---|
| Rank | Pearson correlation | −0.079(*) | −0.097(**) | 0.427(**) | 1 | 0.243(**) | 0.218(**) | 0.094(*) | .247(**) |
| | Significance (two-tailed) | 0.032 | 0.008 | 0.000 | | 0.000 | 0.000 | 0.012 | 0.000 |
| | Sum of squares and cross-products | −330.211 | −359.713 | 223.248 | 1,546.627 | 132.984 | 86.615 | 94.242 | 366.663 |
| | Covariance | −0.445 | −0.485 | 0.301 | 2.084 | 0.180 | 0.117 | 0.131 | 0.515 |
| | N | 743 | 743 | 743 | 743 | 738 | 742 | 718 | 713 |
| Education | Pearson correlation | −0.054 | −0.015 | −0.404(**) | 0.243(**) | 1 | 0.103(**) | 0.086(*) | 0.005 |
| | Significance (two-tailed) | 0.141 | 0.682 | 0.000 | 0.000 | | 0.005 | 0.022 | 0.901 |
| | Sum of squares and cross-products | −80.642 | −19.776 | −75.063 | 132.984 | 195.592 | 14.552 | 30.522 | 2.464 |
| | Covariance | −0.109 | −0.027 | −0.101 | 0.180 | 0.264 | 0.020 | 0.043 | 0.003 |
| | N | 742 | 742 | 742 | 738 | 742 | 741 | 716 | 711 |
| Male | Pearson correlation | −0.041 | −0.016 | 0.037 | 0.218(**) | 0.103(**) | 1 | 0.197(**) | 0.209(**) |
| | Significance (two-tailed) | 0.265 | 0.659 | 0.312 | 0.000 | 0.005 | | 0.000 | 0.000 |
| | Sum of squares and cross-products | −44.392 | −15.513 | 5.031 | 86.615 | 14.552 | 103.416 | 51.096 | 79.953 |
| | Covariance | −0.060 | −0.021 | 0.007 | 0.117 | 0.020 | 0.139 | 0.071 | .112 |
| | N | 747 | 747 | 747 | 742 | 741 | 747 | 722 | 716 |

(continued)

|  |  | OBJECTIVITY INDEX | EFFECTIVENESS INDEX | ANKARA PD | RANK | EDUCATION | MALE | AGE | YEARS OF SERVICE |
|---|---|---|---|---|---|---|---|---|---|
| Age | Pearson correlation | -0.178(**) | -0.057 | -0.404(**) | 0.094(*) | 0.086(*) | 0.197(**) | 1 | 0.829(**) |
|  | Significance (two-tailed) | 0.000 | 0.127 | 0.000 | 0.012 | 0.022 | 0.000 |  | 0.000 |
|  | Sum of squares and cross-products | -488.916 | -137.111 | -136.496 | 94.242 | 30.522 | 51.096 | 674.572 | 816.246 |
|  | Covariance | -0.678 | -0.190 | -0.189 | 0.131 | 0.043 | 0.071 | 0.936 | 1.150 |
|  | N | 722 | 722 | 722 | 718 | 716 | 722 | 722 | 711 |
| Years of service | Pearson correlation | -0.145(**) | -0.044 | -0.196(**) | 0.247(**) | 0.005 | 0.209(**) | 0.829(**) | 1 |
|  | Significance (two-tailed) | 0.000 | 0.240 | 0.000 | 0.000 | 0.901 | 0.000 | 0.000 |  |
|  | Sum of squares and cross-products | -589.285 | -156.247 | -98.071 | 366.663 | 2.464 | 79.953 | 816.246 | 1,483.874 |
|  | Covariance | -0.823 | -0.218 | -0.137 | 0.515 | 0.003 | 0.112 | 1.150 | 2.072 |
|  | N | 717 | 717 | 717 | 713 | 711 | 716 | 711 | 717 |

**, correlation is significant at the 0.01 level (two-tailed); *, correlation is significant at the 0.05 level (two-tailed).

# Index

# A Call for Authors

## Advances in Police Theory and Practice

### AIMS AND SCOPE:

This cutting-edge series is designed to promote publication of books on contemporary advances in police theory and practice. We are especially interested in volumes that focus on the nexus between research and practice, with the end goal of disseminating innovations in policing. We will consider collections of expert contributions as well as individually authored works. Books in this series will be marketed internationally to both academic and professional audiences. This series also seeks to —

- Bridge the gap in knowledge about advances in theory and practice regarding who the police are, what they do, and how they maintain order, administer laws, and serve their communities
- Improve cooperation between those who are active in the field and those who are involved in academic research so as to facilitate the application of innovative advances in theory and practice

The series especially encourages the contribution of works coauthored by police practitioners and researchers. We are also interested in works comparing policing approaches and methods globally, examining such areas as the policing of transitional states, democratic policing, policing and minorities, preventive policing, investigation, patrolling and response, terrorism, organized crime and drug enforcement. In fact, every aspect of policing, public safety and security, as well as public order is relevant for the series. Manuscripts should be between 300 and 600 printed pages. If you have a proposal for an original work or for a contributed volume, please be in touch.

---

**Series Editor**
Dilip Das, Ph.D., Ph: 802-598-3680
E-mail: dilipkd@aol.com

Dr. Das is a professor of criminal justice and Human Rights Consultant to the United Nations. He is a former chief of police and founding president of the International Police Executive Symposium, IPES, www.ipes.info. He is also founding editor-in-chief of *Police Practice and Research: An International Journal* (PPR) (Routledge/Taylor & Francis), www.tandf.co.uk/journals. In addition to editing the *World Police Encyclopedia* (Taylor & Francis, 2006), Dr. Das has published numerous books and articles during his many years of involvement in police practice, research, writing, and education.

**Proposals for the series may be submitted to the series editor or directly to —**
Carolyn Spence
Senior Editor • CRC Press / Taylor & Francis Group
561-998-2515 • 561-997-7249 (fax)
carolyn.spence@taylorandfrancis.com • www.crcpress.com
6000 Broken Sound Parkway NW, Suite 300, Boca Raton, FL 33487

For Product Safety Concerns and Information please contact our EU
representative GPSR@taylorandfrancis.com
Taylor & Francis Verlag GmbH, Kaufingerstraße 24, 80331 München, Germany

www.ingramcontent.com/pod-product-compliance
Ingram Content Group UK Ltd.
Pitfield, Milton Keynes, MK11 3LW, UK
UKHW021610240425
457818UK00018B/486

* 9 7 8 0 3 6 7 8 6 5 3 2 0 *